"What an outstanding book of hope and comfort. A must-read for every counselor counseling a grieving, hurting heart. Connie ministers such tender compassion and graciousness to those drowning in their sea of grief. She reminds us of our 'Life Preserver, Jesus Christ,' who is always there to rescue us in the darkness of our raging storm.

"She drives home God's sovereignty, and in neon lights throughout her journey points us to the One and only Person who can provide the hope and comfort that restores our hearts, our source of all true comfort in this sin-cursed life, Jesus Christ, our Savior.

"Connie's goal was to grieve in a way as to glorify God in the grieving process. You did, Sister; you have lived and written how to restore broken hearts to a biblical pattern, using the wisdom and comfort of God's awesome Word. Thank you for sharing your journey. This book will definitely be recommended to other counselors and hurting hearts."

—*Katherine Pell*
Certified NANC Counselor

"There is much suffering and grief in our world today, and I am touched by one very special sister in Christ whom the Lord has placed in my life, the author of this book. Connie has a gentle and quiet spirit and a tender heart for those who are suffering through grief. She deeply understands the depths of despair and grief after losing her beloved husband. The Lord has given her great courage to share her story, her heart, and her journeys with those the Lord leads to read her book. I've served with Connie in Bible Study Fellowship as her teaching leader and have noted tremendous spiritual growth in Connie since she first started leadership. What strikes me most about Connie is her genuine concern for others. She listens to others with her heart and seizes opportunities to encourage and come alongside them. Anyone going through grief or knowing someone who has a grieving loved one will benefit from her book. I've already placed into practice some of the helpful tips the Lord has given Connie. May you find God's comfort and encouragement through her words."

—*Debbie Walker*
Teaching Leader, Bible Study Fellowship

Grieving
for the
Glory of God

Is There a Tomorrow?

CONNIE SUMMERS

WestBow Press
P R E S S
A DIVISION OF THOMAS NELSON

The information, ideas, and suggestions in this book are not intended as a substitute for professional advice. Before following any suggestions contained in this book, you should consult your personal physician or mental health professional. You should not undertake any diet/ exercise regimen recommended in this book before consulting your personal physician.

Neither the author nor the publisher shall be liable or responsible for any loss or damage allegedly arising as a consequence of your use or application of any information or suggestions in this book.

WestBow Press books may be ordered through booksellers or by contacting:

WestBow Press
A Division of Thomas Nelson
1663 Liberty Drive
Bloomington, IN 47403
www.westbowpress.com
1-(866) 928-1240

Because of the dynamic nature of the Internet, any web addresses or links contained in this book may have changed since publication and may no longer be valid. The views expressed in this work are solely those of the author and do not necessarily reflect the views of the publisher, and the publisher hereby disclaims any responsibility for them.

Any people depicted in stock imagery provided by Thinkstock are models, and such images are being used for illustrative purposes only.

Certain stock imagery © Thinkstock.

ISBN: 978-1-4497-4380-2 (hc)
ISBN: 978-1-4497-4379-6 (sc)
ISBN: 978-1-4497-4378-9 (e)

Library of Congress Control Number: 2012905136

Printed in the United States of America

WestBow Press rev. date: 04/03/2012

Contents

In loving memory of Bud:
Beloved Husband, Dad, and PapPaw

And to
Jesus Christ,
my beloved Savior

Who is he, this King of glory?
The L<small>ORD</small> Almighty—
he is the King of glory. Selah

(Psalm 24:10)

Preface

$\mathcal{W}$hy write a book about grieving the loss of a spouse? Numerous books expounding the importance of grieving have already been written, and these give all kinds of advice: how to grieve; what, or what not, to expect; whether to seek help from others; whether to grieve alone, as it is a solitary process. The list goes on and on. In addition, there are many books written by biblical authorities. Many of these books are excellent resources filled with helpful information.

The question remains, why write this book? It is because I have experienced my husband's dying; I know the turmoil and discouragement it brings. I have experienced the uncontrollable ups and downs that occur. I know what helped and what hindered my healing. Also, I have an earnest desire to share my knowledge and experiences with others.

In several ways, my grief affected other people. Most of them, although well meaning, did not know how to respond to me or how to help me heal and adjust to a new life. This book will provide guidance to those of you who are seeking to comfort, support, and encourage a grieving person.

If you are that grieving person, you will find that grieving is not a passive process. There are personal actions to take and changes to make. As you travel with me on my journey, I will lead you to God's Word. There, together, we will find all the instructions, truths, and promises we need.

I urge anyone who may be grieving to read this book. There are many amazing discoveries you will find to help you out of the depths of your grief. This book offers down-to-earth help, when down-to-earth help is what you need.

It is my hope that this book will serve as a witness to the wonderful works of Jesus Christ, our Lord and Savior. If you do not know Jesus personally, the plan of salvation is found at the end of this book.

A final note: My expressed suffering (past and present) is not about sympathizing with me. It is about others seeing the power of God working through my weaknesses, as demonstrated throughout this book.

Most important, you will see our Most Holy God's magnificent attributes, and all the glory will be his.

You are worthy, our Lord and God, to receive glory and honor
and power, for you created all things, and by your will they
were created and have their being.
(Revelation 4:11)

Introduction

$\mathcal{I}$ felt there was a need for a book that could relate a firsthand account of grief as experienced by the left-behind spouse. My inspiration came as I began to reread past journal entries. These entries led me through a grieving journey into a spiritual journey of healing. I invite you to tag along on my journey, as I relate the many personal struggles that led to my victory over a sad, grieving heart.

My desire is to share with you what helped and what hindered my healing. Although this is a unique opportunity for me, it's one that leaves me quite vulnerable, as I will be sharing many serious and private moments. Remember that these are my thoughts, feelings, and emotions—mine alone.

The personal notations are from journal entries, my own written prayers, and/or numerous jottings and quick scribbles here and there. I share these with an open and sincere heart. My prayer is that you will find the hope in God's Word as I did.

The knowledge content was obtained from the Holy Bible, New International Version (NIV,) unless otherwise stated; also from various resource books, numerous Bible studies, Pastor's sermons, Sunday school lessons, counseling sessions, and mentoring from biblical friends.

Both journeys (grieving and spiritual) are filled with entries relating to the extreme ups and downs that are experienced when a person is in the depths of grief.

The spiritual journey also includes Scriptures, lessons, and applications. The Scriptures will point to the truth of God's Word (the Bible), and his promises. The lessons are what God is teaching through his Word. The applications are intended to help you apply God's Word to your daily living.

Writing this book has been a great challenge for me. Never having written professionally, I was intimidated by the magnitude of this project. I felt ill equipped and unsure of my ability. I sought God and asked for guidance and help. There I left it in his hands. God blessed me. As I relived my journey, I gained knowledge and wisdom, grew spiritually, and gained valuable insight. I now walk closer to God than ever before. I pray that you too will have a similar outcome.

It is my hope that, whether you have a personal relationship with God or not, this book will show you the awesome power and strength God gives to grieving persons. You will discover his marvelous promises and let them heal you from the inside out. You will find hope, encouragement, and comfort from a living, loving God. Every grieving heart needs God!

My sincere thanks to all who encouraged, supported, and assisted me in the writing of this book.

May God's blessings be upon each of you.

—C. S.

Part I

The Past—Bud's Illness

Thoughts of the Past

My thoughts are going back to the past. These thoughts take me to the years of Bud's illness and death. Grief tries hard to penetrate the rock-hard shell I've placed around my heart. If only these terrible thoughts would go away. I don't want to think about the past, but I do! I let the memories come quickly and rapidly, like water rushing over a dam. Once one tear falls, there is no shutting off the dam. The flood is just minutes away.

I shut my flooded eyes and let the memories float by—one after another, after another, after another . . .

Years of Bud's Illness

I'm thinking back through the years. I get stuck at 1981 when Bud had his first heart catheterization. We received a good report—only slight plaque buildup. How thankful we were.

The next few years were busy years. The kids graduated and moved away from home; Bud and I traveled some; I retired; and several grandchildren were born. We opened our hearts and home to my mom and Bud's mom, as their health declined and they needed care. Our parents passed away. During those years, there were many joyous happenings and some real struggles and difficulties.

The next medical milestone was in 1988 when Bud was diagnosed with hypertension. He started taking medication for the first time. In 2000 Bud had another heart catheterization, requiring a balloon procedure. Two years later, he had plaque in two heart arteries removed.

Life continued, and as the seasons came and went, we managed to weather the ups and downs. It seemed as each season changed, Bud's health changed also. The years from 2000 to 2002 brought many changes resulting in new diagnoses: congestive heart failure, chronic obstructive pulmonary disease (emphysema), peripheral arterial disease (requiring surgery twice), and cardiovascular disease (requiring placement of stents). In 2003, he was diagnosed with gout. He also had cancer of the bladder that year. Two years later, he had lung cancer. Both cancers were treated with radiation. In 2004, one artery in his heart had a 100 percent blockage, and another had a 99 percent blockage; he again required stents. In 2005, he was diagnosed with neuropathy. He also had a constriction of the esophagus, which required frequent stretching and injections of Botox.

With each new diagnosis came physical problems: failing eyesight, balance problems, unsteady gait with frequent falling, bowel problems, an occasional TIA (small stroke), chronic pain from a previous back injury, neuropathy, impaired memory and judgment, and changes in personality. There were numerous appointments, procedures, lab workups, and tests. In 2005 his heart function was 30 percent and his lung function was 42 percent, and these never improved. Many, many times, Bud was taken to the emergency room and/or hospitalized, frequently with pneumonia. Of course, with each new diagnosis came new medication and problems with drug interactions. By 2007, he required continuous oxygen.

The period of time from January to August 2008 is difficult to describe, for Bud had good days. He was able to drive once in a while, only around Augusta, but he would tell me he frequently had trouble finding his way home. Some days, although it was a tremendous struggle, he was able to climb stairs. Occasionally he would even attempt to mow the lawn, but was unable. The desire was there but not the physical strength. In April of 2008 the changes began to come more quickly. I could see some medical and physical regression each day. In June and July, he had several TIAs (mini strokes), often with falling and some short-term effects. In August the massive strokes accrued.

Walking with Jesus

April 2005

In 2005, Bud's health began to fluctuate; it would improve and then decline for the next three years. My situation and circumstances did not change. I began to change. I knew the Holy Spirit was leading and guiding me. God was watching over me. I began my daily, steady walk with Jesus.

The words of a favorite hymn come to mind.

Just a Closer Walk with Thee

I am weak but Thou art strong
Jesus, keep me from all wrong.
I'll be satisfied as long
As I walk, let me walk close to Thee.

Refrain: Just a closer walk with Thee, Grant it, Jesus is my plea.
Daily walking close to Thee, Let it be, dear Lord, let it be.
(The Celebration Hymnal, Word/Integrity, 1997))

God Answers Prayer, and Provides

April 2008

The doctor has just discharged Bud after his leg bypass surgery. I remind him that Bud's potassium level was 2.2. I know this is a dangerously low level. He tells me it will come up. Bud has had problems with both low and high levels in the past.

As the doctor walks out the door, I just sit down and cry, asking God to carry this burden for me. It is just too much for me. I don't know what I will do if the potassium continues to drop after we get home.

Just as I'm finishing my prayer, Bud's cardiologist walks in. He says he is here just to pay a courtesy visit. I tell him about Bud's potassium level. He tells me to increase his dose to twelve pills a day for two days and then taper it off each day until back to normal dose. I thank him and then remind him that I cannot determine level without a blood test.

He writes out an order for blood work PRN (whenever necessary). He says to me, "You can decide when it is needed, as you know what to look for." He adds to the lab order: "At the wife's discretion." (I am an RN.)

God is great. He heard my prayer and answered it in a way I didn't expect. He provided for Bud's needs and mine also: "If you believe, you will receive whatever you ask for in prayer" (Matthew 21:22).

My Life During Bud's Long Illness

uring the years of Bud's illness (eight years), it was very difficult for me, and I suffered as I watched him suffer. For three years, I took complete care of him and at the same time kept up the house, yard, bills, etc. There were many doctor's appointments, treatments, procedures, tests, etc., which averaged five to six a month. But despite all this, I was in a familiar, steadfast, almost comfortable place.

I was walking close to God, trusting in him, and hanging on to every promise. Every morning, God blessed me with quiet time. Bud usually slept until about 9:00, and I would get up at 6:00. I would use that time to study for Bible Study Fellowship, study the Bible on my own, and read daily devotions. I read many, many spiritual and resource books. My pastor gave me copies of his sermons, and I would review them. When I sat with Bud, I usually read the Psalms. I felt I was obeying God's Word.

In 2008 everything started to shift and change. It was like God was leading me into unknown territory, away from my familiar, comfortable daily routine and schedule. I wanted to hang on to the familiar. I wondered what was happening. I knew Bud was having small strokes and occasionally more severe ones. Prior to this, he had been willing to go to the doctor, although he was always reluctant to go to the hospital. Being an RN, I knew that I could continue to take care of him, medically and physically.

Questions were swirling around in my head. As I prayed, I asked God, "What will be happening in the days ahead? You know, God, Bud's condition has always stabilized before. Will it this time? Please, God, don't let him have another bad stroke. What do you expect from me? Please stay close to me and give me strength and endurance; I will do whatever you ask of me. And keep me focused on you, my almighty God."

One day, during my quiet time, I read that when Jesus brings out his own sheep, He goes before them, and the sheep follow Him. "My sheep listen to my voice; I know them, and they follow me" (John 10:27).

I knew Jesus was leading me, and I knew I needed to follow. I was fearful; I doubted I could do all he was asking. I picked up my Bible again and found another truth: Jesus will never lead me down a path that is too dangerous. He will always be there to help me. He knows how much I can handle. He knows the way to green pastures. All he was asking of me was to follow him.

I clung to these truths as Bud's condition continued to decline. And I hung on with both hands, as Bud suffered two massive strokes in August.

Back of Notebook

These are some jottings I wrote on the back cover of the notebook in which I wrote an hour-by-hour assessment of Bud during the last two weeks. These are my thoughts (except number nine):

1. Is there a tomorrow?
2. Should we come?
3. Where are my answers?
4. If I can do anything, just call.
5. Let me know how he is doing.
6. What about me?
7. Remain at home or move to medical facility. 106 pounds versus 190 pounds.
8. God's miraculous timing and provision.
9. "Hold my hand." (Bud speaking)
10. Denied visit.
11. After everyone goes home. The hours from 6:00 p.m. to 9:00 a.m.
12. It's really the little things that matter.
13. Being restless. Being anxious versus being snowed with drugs.
14. What does "keep him comfortable" mean?
15. I want to get out of the RN business and just be a wife and caregiver.
16. Remember the Kleenex.
17. The dreaded diagnosis.
18. Where did my bed go?
19. My hours in the chair, and now on the couch, just watching him breathe.
20. Put into the system.
21. The things people say.
22. Finally an answer—now what do I do?

[AUTHOR'S NOTE: *My daughter, Teresa, stayed with me the last ten days. And my cousin, Katie, was here most days the last week; she also stayed some nights. Both were a tremendous blessing to me. They helped me through many difficult times, and we were even able to laugh a little.*]

Bud Is Saved

*M*y dear heavenly Father, Lord, and Savior,

My prayer this morning is the same as it has been for years; please call Bud to be one of you on your own. I know each day brings more changes in his condition. The little strokes are more frequent. When he fell last night, I had to let him stay on the floor until he knew who I was. He had no strength to help me get him in the chair. I know you gave me the strength I needed. It was very hard. This is the worst he has been. Even after getting in the chair, it was several hours before he was able to carry on a conversation with me or hold his own glass. Of course, Father, you already know all this.

I know Bud has listened to me and has asked questions about the Bible. But only minimally; he still won't listen about being saved. Why is he so stubborn? He has even let me pray each night with him over the last couple of years. I know he listens when I pray, as he often will ask questions when I finish. Please, Father!

August 8, 2008

Pastor has come to talk to Bud. I didn't tell Bud he was coming. Dear Lord, it is up to you. Please make Bud listen and understand. I know you can change hearts that are hardened. And I know you will change Bud's.

Pastor is starting to talk. Bud doesn't look up at Pastor. I tell him, "Bud, look at Pastor; he is talking to you." I know my voice is very firm, and Bud is not used to that. Immediately Bud looks at Pastor, and I know he is listening. Thank you, Father.

As Pastor leaves, I follow him, asking, "Do think he understood and is saved?"

Pastor replies, "We'll see what kind of fruit he produces."

I'm disappointed. I wonder to myself, *What kind of fruit can he produce? He isn't able to even move without help.*

But then I recall a verse in Romans which lifts my spirits.

And those he predestined, he also called; those he called, he also justified; those he justified, he also glorified.
(Romans 8:30)

After that day, Bud never showed anger, never swore, and was never hostile or threatening. He was gentle and even began to thank me for little things.

[AUTHOR'S NOTE: *Bud became a different person in many ways after the TIAs and major strokes. His personality changed a great deal. His mind was confused. He did not think in the same way as he had before. His behavior and speech also changed.*]

August 12, 2008

Today has been normal. Bud has been in and out of bed, several times. It is getting harder to get him into bed each time. I know I couldn't do it without God and Teresa.

Time for prayers. Teresa is on one side of the bed; I am on the other. Bud, Teresa, and I all hold hands. When I finish praying I say "Amen," and Teresa repeats "Amen." I lean very close to Bud and say "Amen," trying to prompt Bud to say it also. His eyes open, and he says "hallelujah." We are all smiling. Thank you, Jesus.

Later Teresa and I are just sitting, relaxing a little before going to bed. Bud says something.

Teresa says, "Did you hear that? Dad said, 'Jesus is watching me.'"

I go to the bed and say, "Bud did you say that Jesus is watching you?"

Bud says, "Yes, he is."

I tell him, "Yes, Jesus is watching you, and soon you will be in heaven with him. And one day I will be there with you and Jesus." Tears of thankfulness and joy fall from my eyes.

Salvation is found in no one else, for there is no name
under heaven given to men by which we must be saved.
(Acts 4:12)

Everyone who calls on the name of the Lord will be saved.
(Romans 10:13)

Part II

Bud's Death
and
Days That Followed

The Day Bud Dies

August 15, 2008

Teresa and her son, Tanner, are still sleeping. I know these last ten days have been very hard for her. She has put her own life on hold in order to come here to be with me and help care for her dad. So I let her sleep. I sit, as I have all night, watching Bud. The medication has been effective; he is no longer agitated and restless. God's blessing. I sip my coffee and hear Bud's breathing become more labored. He starts to gurgle. These sounds are known as the "death rattles"; I know this. I murmur a short prayer that God will take him soon—that his suffering will be over. I ask God for strength and endurance for myself.

My heart is breaking and my tears are falling as I give him the meds to dry up his secretions. I know it is time to call the hospice RN, just for notification, but I hesitate. I can't dial the number. I don't want to say the words. It makes death too real. I am not prepared. I'll just wait; maybe he will respond to the meds.

Am I imagining things? It has only been a short time. No, it isn't my imagination. His breathing is more labored, and the secretions drool from his mouth. Without any further hesitation, I call hospice. She tells me to give him more meds and asks if I want her to come. I tell her, "No, not yet."

I pray again that God will help me just get through today, and I thank him for Bud's salvation. I gently lay a cool cloth on Bud's forehead. I don't know why I do this; there is no fever. I'm thinking this is the only comfort I can give him. I give him more meds and try to read the Twenty-third Psalm. But I can't concentrate. I'm so very cold. I don't want to be alone, but I don't want to wake Teresa either. I just sit and stare. The only thought I have is, *Bud is really going to die, be taken away from me. Now my mind is totally blank.*

17

I am crying softly when Teresa and Tanner get up. I pretend I am okay and Bud is too. I don't want to upset or frighten them. Later in the morning, Teresa runs some errands. Katie, my cousin, comes. I ask Katie to go to the drugstore for me. She leaves.

Tanner wants to make potato salad. We are in the kitchen. I can see Bud from the kitchen. Every two to three minutes I check on Bud. I sit beside the hospital bed, reach out, and touch his face.

I am showing Tanner how to cut the celery. Something stirs inside me, and my heart seems to stop. I know this is the end. I go to his bed, as if in a trance. I hold his hand and whisper so quietly that only Bud can hear me. "You will never know how much I have loved you. You were my first and only love, and we really did have a good marriage. I will miss you, but I will see you in heaven." I hold on tight to his hand, and in that same moment, he is gone. I sit for a few minutes, not wanting to let go.

Then I say to Tanner, "PapPaw is really getting sicker. Will you please go outdoors till Mama gets back?" He goes out the back door, through the garage. His shoe slips, and he cuts his foot on the step. I hear a gentle knock on the door and Tanner's tiny whisper, "MamMaw I'm sorry to bother you. Can you look at my toe?" His toe is bleeding profusely. I send him to the front porch, where I clean and bandage his toe.

I return to Bud, putting my cheek near his mouth to feel his breath. I can't feel any air, so I listen with my stethoscope for a heartbeat, which can't be heard. I gently kiss his forehead, his last kiss from me, tears streaming down my face.

As Katie comes in the door, I say, "Katie, he's gone." She hugs me, and we cry and cry.

The hospice nurse comes. The men from the funeral home come to remove the body. My mind cannot grasp what is happening. The form laying on the gurney isn't Bud. It's just a mass, a bulge. *Please God, help me feel something. Don't let my heart turn cold and bitter.*

At that moment, something snaps inside me. I am numb, but I realize something strange and frightening is happening within my mind. Feelings and emotions are gone, replaced by a need to get things done in an orderly and appropriate way. I tell myself I know what has to be done, and I will do it. There are people to be called and arrangements to be made. I refuse to have anyone feel sorry for me. To think I am incapable. I am in autopilot mode. Just watch me go! My mind tells me, *Do not be a weak, self-pitying, self-centered woman. I am strong and competent.*

Where is God at this moment? I wonder.

Bud's Things

August 15, 2008, Evening

𝓑utch and Nancy, my brother and sister-in-law are here. The men have come to take the hospital bed away. The oxygen company has removed the oxygen condenser and all those extra tanks and supplies. I look around, and Butch and Nancy have rearranged my furniture. It is now back where it was a few years ago. I never thought this day would come.

I know they are trying to be helpful. And I appreciate their care and concern. I just watch. "Thank you," Crying will come later. Butch and Nancy leave. I guess everything is done.

I'm alone until Teresa comes back. I look around. This morning I just did not realize that by this afternoon most of Bud's things would be gone. And that this morning was the last time I would see Bud's things arranged where he could see them and use them. The bedding gone from the couch, the hospital bed gone, the commode gone, the walker gone, the electric scooter gone, the oxygen gone.

Bud is gone!

Everything is now down in the basement, already in storage. I know this has to be, but it just hurts so much to think Bud's things can be moved out of sight so quickly and easily. The only thing that remains is the tray of medication on the table, his glasses, nail clippers, and a few little personal items. His clothes and personal things are still in the bedroom. The flannel shirts and coats are in the hall closet. His canes are there also. His boots are in the garage.

I go to his closet in the bedroom. All his shirts, jeans, and even a suit hang there. I move a few things and find his hunting coat, with his gloves still stuffed in the pocket. He was always planning to go hunting next year.

Further into the closet I find his Navy uniform. My tears flow uncontrollably now as I remember the first time I saw him: he was home on leave from the Navy. I hear Teresa come in, and I shut off the light and close the door.

A door has also closed in my life. A door that can never be opened again.

Funeral Week

*A*ll my family and friends have been notified. I yell at Katie because she is using my phone to call long distance. We laugh about it. But I really don't care if I hurt her feelings. What is wrong with me? I am not thinking about anyone or anything right now; I just want to get through the next few days.

Teresa and I make funeral arrangements. We pick out flowers. Relatives—Bud's family—arrive from Illinois. Food is brought to the house, and we eat often. I'm never hungry anymore. Everyone tells me I've lost too much weight. I don't care. The agony is so raw, so deep, I simply cannot bring myself to care.

Bud's son, Mike, arrives from Florida with his family. The house is filled with people, and at times there is laughter. I don't care; I only pretend I do. It is getting easier and easier to just pretend than to have to face reality.

Greg, Bud's cousin's son, gathers us on the deck. He wants input from everyone, as he is preparing the eulogy. I don't pay much attention; when someone laughs, I laugh too. I don't care. I do add one thing about Bud and his love for kids; I relate a couple of stories.

I tell my cousin, Shirley, that I would like her daughter-in-law, Sue, to sing. Sue agrees. Greg and Pastor meet to go over the eulogy.

Before Visitation

*W*hat I'm unable to verbalize what I need most? Before leaving for the funeral home, I just need someone to take me aside and sit close to me. Remind me of Bud's salvation. Let me relate his testimony, even if I have related it before.

I need someone to read Scripture to me.

> For it is by grace you have been saved, through faith—and this not from yourselves, it is the gift of God—not by works, so that no one can boast.
>
> (Ephesians 2:8, 9)

This verse is so comforting and reassuring to me.

As we walk into the funeral home, I need someone to remind me again that Bud was saved. And then as I look upon Bud, lying in the casket, I need someone to say to me, "This is only a physical reminder of Bud. Bud is rejoicing with the angels and walking with Jesus in heaven. He will be waiting for you, Connie."

> In my Father's house are many rooms; if it were not so, I would have told you. I am going there to prepare a place for you. And if I go and prepare a place for you, I will come back and take you to be with me that you also may be where I am.
>
> (John 14:2, 3)

Finally I need someone to say a little prayer (silently or out loud) for me and my family.

Visitation

It is time to get ready for visitation. I have to get dressed. I don't know what to wear. It's just so hard to make a decision about anything. And it doesn't even matter anyway, what I wear.

The family is to arrive first; that's good I guess. I just don't want to go at all. The visitation is like all visitations. People come and people go. They say, "Oh, he looks good" and "Well, he isn't suffering anymore." They turn their attention to other people who are standing around, looking uncomfortable, and wanting to leave. They look around, and some find other people they know and can talk with. Most leave without saying good-bye to me or my family. I feel like I'm suffering alone, hardly knowing how to compose myself. I just want to stay near the casket where Bud lies. I just can't grieve openly.

My Actual Thoughts While at Visitation

We arrive at the funeral home. Only family is here right now. I go to the casket. He looks so young; all the effects of his long illness are gone. I just have to smooth the cuff of his sweater, even though it isn't wrinkled. My hand brushes his, and I feel only cold lifeless skin. A slight smile comes unexpectedly as I remember how his huge warm fingers would completely swallow up my hand whenever we held hands while walking in the woods.

Too soon other people begin to arrive. Now is the time to smile, but a deep sadness covers me as I stand at the casket, too numb to move. I refuse to cry. A deep sorrowful sigh slips from my mouth as I step back and turn to face the mass of people. My head and heart are twisted together like a tangled ball of yarn. *Think, think! Pay attention, and remember who's here and what's happening right now.* I can't stay in the present; my mind travels back to Bud and caring for him. I hear people speaking to me, but the haze in my mind is so thick, I'm unable to respond with words. I just nod my head. I am helpless and defenseless. I can't let anyone come too close. Someone is coming over, and it seems they are talking to me, telling me he looks good. I nod and say yes. More people come toward me saying, those dreaded words, "Well, at least he isn't suffering anymore."

A friend of Bud's comes toward me, and I manage to say a few words to him. "Hello, thanks for coming. Bud thought a lot of you and talked about you often."

"Come on, Connie. Come sit down." *Don't pull my arm! Don't make me sit down. Don't you understand? If I sit down I will never get back up again.*

Someone sits me next to Uncle Franz. *Talk to him, thank him for coming, and ask how he is doing.* I do my best, and then I stand up.

I move around the room, going from person to person and saying, "Thanks for coming." I answer their questions: "Yes, he does look good." "No, he isn't suffering anymore." "Yes, I'll stay in my house." "Yes, I'm doing okay." "No, I don't need anything." "Yes, the funeral will be hard, but I'm okay." "Of course, I can rest now." "No, I'm not tired." "No, I don't need to sit down." "Good to see you too; sure, I'll give you a call." "Yes, the flowers are pretty."

What time is it? I wonder. *Where are Teresa and her boys, Terry Lee and Tanner? Where are Mike and Jonalyn (Mike's wife)? Where is Scott (my son)? Dear Lord, find them for me; they should not have left already. I can't keep track of them. Where are they?*

"Hi, thanks for coming," I say to someone else. "Yes, the flowers are nice. Thanks for sending them."

Oh, where are those kids? Oh, there they are; they didn't leave after all. Only family is left.

"Mom, Mom," Teresa is holding my arm. "Everyone has left. Are you ready to go?"

No, I really want to stay close to your dad, to just look upon him and remember. But I know I must go. I tell Teresa, "Okay, I'm ready. Are people coming to the house?" *Please God, let people come. I don't want to be alone.* "Yes, Mom, everyone is coming." *Oh no! Dear God, I don't want to have to talk to anyone.*

The Funeral

August 19, 2008

*I*t's really cold today for August. Everyone who stayed here last night is out on the deck, standing together and talking. I guess I should have fixed some breakfast, not just coffee. Maybe they made some toast. Too late now. Teresa and the boys have just arrived. The boys look so nice, all dressed up and wearing ties. Mike and Jonalyn haven't come yet. Pete, David, and Dottie (Bud's cousin and his children) have now come also. Pete is not feeling well, so Dottie is taking him home to Illinois. I hope he feels better. Butch and Nancy are here now. It's time to go.

My Memories of the Funeral:

I remember Bud's sister, Mary, and her husband, Wilb, coming in the door. I went to them, and we talked a little. Others came and seated themselves. I was so nervous, I was shaking. I remember Mike asking where his family should sit. I said, "Please sit right behind me." I know Teresa and Tanner sat on my right and Scott and Terry Lee sat on my left. The couch was very crowded.

Greg read the eulogy, and Pastor gave the sermon. During Pastor's sermon the large blanket of flowers fell off Bud's casket. There was a small rumble of laughter. *My thought was: God has a sense of humor, and He wanted His presence to be known and felt.*

After the funeral we went to Fort Custer National Cemetery, where Bud was to be buried. I remember going to other funerals at Fort Custer. They honor fallen fellow servicemen or—women. There is a gun salute, and they present a flag to the surviving spouse or family member. I was crying uncontrollably; I did not even realize when they handed me the flag. Pastor closed in prayer, and Sue sang "Our Father". It was beautiful.

There was a luncheon at church, prepared by the ladies. There was an abundance of food. I went from table to table, in a fog. I do not remember who was there.

I cannot recall anything about the evening once we returned home.

Hurtful Things Said

Many things were said to me which were very hurtful, causing me anguish and sorrow. Most of these words were spoken at visitation, at the funeral, or shortly after the funeral; however, some were said several months later. I know many of them were said with intended sincerity and kindness. But each person speaking did not understand how I would interpret these words. I know my feelings were too close to the surface.

I am including these to help you know what to say—and what not to say—when you speak to a person who has lost a spouse. I heard all these things from more than one person.

1. **Time will heal.** (This was the thing most often said.)

    I wanted to ask them, "What do you mean? What will time heal? Me? Am I broken? How long will it take? When will I know it is 'healed'?"

2. **It just takes time.** (This is similar to "time will heal," and it was the thing second most often said.)

    I wanted to ask, "What is the 'it' everyone is talking about? And how much time should I give 'it'? Are you giving me a guarantee I'll be okay? How do you know I was okay before? And how do you measure okay?"

3. **It was God's will.** (Christians most often say this.)

    I know this. And I know what it means. But I wanted to ask, "Why don't you take time with me to talk about God's will?"

4. **Just call if you need anything.** (This is what people say when they want to take the easy way out.)

    I wanted to say, "What I really think you are saying is, 'I need to say something that sounds nice, but I don't really have time for you.'"

28

5. I'll visit when everything is over. (This promise was broken more often than not.)

   I remember this, even though it was said at the gravesite. And I remember all of you who said it still haven't visited. I guess everything isn't over yet.

6. You had a lot of time to prepare for this, with him being sick for so long. (This was the most uncaring thing I heard.)

   I wanted to tell them, "First, the 'him' you speak of is Bud. Please use his name. Bud was a person. And my husband. And you say I had a lot of time to prepare. For what? Do you really think this helps? I am thinking you're telling me I should have been expecting this, so there is nothing more to do or say."

7. You've just got to get over it yourself. (Only one person said this, but it really hurt.)

   I was too hurt to even respond, but what I would have liked to say was, "Sure, okay, I'm over it. You are off the hook; nothing more you need to say or do."

8. Now you can do whatever you want to. (I think the people who said this really did mean well.)

   I wanted to explain, "What you don't understand is, I want to take care of and love my husband. Have him here with me. At this time, nothing else matters."

9. You have freedom from having to take care of Bud. (Similar to number 8.)

   "At least you used his name," I wanted to say. "But I don't want that kind of freedom; I want Bud."

10. You took such good care of Bud; you have nothing to feel guilty about. (There were several variations of this.)

    This made me want to shoot back, "Who said I feel guilty? I do not. I did take excellent care of Bud."

11. What will you do with your house? You can't take care of it by yourself. (This shows concern only for material things.)

    I almost wanted to laugh. "You don't know it, but I've been taking care of it completely for the last four years. But I am not explaining that to you."

12. Don't make any major decisions for six months. (This is what the "advice givers" said, not knowing what else to say.)

I just wanted to scream, "Make major decisions?! I couldn't even decide what to wear today. And I did not ask for your advice."

13. At least he isn't suffering anymore. (This was an attempt to comfort me.)

I wanted to tell them, "No he isn't, but I am."

14. I know how you feel; I've been there. (This was the least helpful of all.)

I wanted to shout, "What do you mean, you've been there? Were you married to Bud? Really, I think you are self-centered and just want to talk about yourself."

[AUTHOR'S NOTE: *So many times I thought people were just trying to say something helpful, but did not know what to say. They relied on things they had heard others say. I really do not think anyone said things to deliberately hurt me. They just did not understand how much I was hurting and how confused I was.*]

Helpful Things to Say

Let me now offer some words that are comforting and encouraging to those grieving. Some of these are the same or similar to the ones in the previous list, but said with a vastly different intention and focus. Remember too that words aren't always necessary; just being close is often enough. Silence often speaks louder than words.

1. **Time will heal.** (It really isn't necessary to talk about time, so consider carefully before saying this.)

    If you are close to the griever, you can say that time is a healer. But also that the pain and hurt may never go away completely. It may become less painful, and people heal in their own time—and God's. Encourage grievers to take as long as they need to grieve.

    If you do talk about time, wait for two to four weeks after the funeral. At the time of the funeral, it is just too difficult to relate to time at all. All the grievers' thoughts are on the funeral and those first few days alone.

2. **It just takes time; you'll be okay.** (Similar to number one.)

    If you truly love and care about those grieving, do not say this. True, it takes time, but to those grieving, "okay" may never happen. And when grievers think of time, it means being alone for the rest of their lives. They need you to listen, to hear their thoughts, feelings, and concerns.

3. **It was God's will.**

    If you want to talk about God's will, find time alone with those grieving. Open the Bible and read to them. You may know a Scripture to talk about. The Twenty-third Psalm is always an encouraging one. Don't just read, though; talk about God's Word. Come back later to talk some more about God's will.

4. **Just call if you need anything.**
Show the grievers that you really do care by telling them *when* you will be calling—tomorrow, the next day, in a week, or whenever. Give them something to look forward to. And then do it. When you do call, ask specific questions. "Can I help you do _____?" "Do you need groceries? I can get them for you, or would you like to go with me?" "I would like to visit. When is a good time?" "Let's go out for lunch or to a movie." Offer to do the things you used to do together, and then set a date.
Other questions you can ask include "Have you been walking? Let's plan on getting together to take a walk. I need the exercise." These are only suggestions; you know them. You know what they like to do; you know their hobbies and interests. If you do not know them really well, ask what they like to do. Stop by with a magazine or book. If you leave it up to the grievers to call you, it will never happen.

5. **I'll visit when everything is over.**
Never say you will do something and then not do it. It is a promise broken. Don't ask the grievers to make a commitment for a future get-together at the gravesite or the funeral luncheon; they won't remember. If you really want to get together, you must be responsible for making the call.

6. **You had a lot of time to prepare for this, with him being sick for so long.**
You need to know that no matter what the circumstances of a death may be, no one is ever really prepared for the actual death. Come visit with the grievers and let them tell you about their spouses, sharing what they choose to about the illness. Most grievers have so much they would like to talk about. All the years of illness were not filled with sadness. (The eight years of Bud's illness weren't. We had some joyous and happy times. And a few funny incidents that I would love to talk about. We had thirty-eight years of marriage, without illness. This is likely the case for other grieving spouses.)

7. **I know how you feel. I've been there.** (I cannot put this in strong enough words: *Don't ever say this. Don't even imply this.*)
You can sit with the grievers and ask if they want to talk about their feelings. And then let them speak without interruption. There

may come a time when the grievers ask you how you managed to get through your grief if you have lost a spouse. Or they may even ask you for help. But not right away.

8. You can do whatever you want do. (Don't say this. It implies the grievers were not doing what they wanted to do.)

From my perspective, I was ministering to my husband with love and serving God. Nothing else that I will ever do will compare with that. Talk to those grieving about how they can still serve God and care for others. After so much time spent as a caregiver, they feel a void. I felt, "No one needs me now."

9. You have freedom from having to take care of Bud. (Don't say this. It's a worthless statement.)

I'm not sure why anyone would say this. But several did. It sounded to me like they thought I was in prison, having to care for Bud. And I would rather be caring for him than have any kind of freedom. The kind of freedom you speak of is a painful one to those grieving.

10. You took such good care of Bud; you have nothing to feel guilty about.

I felt, "Yes, tell me I took good care of Bud, because I did." So, yes, tell those grieving that they were excellent caregivers. But there is no need to add anything about guilt. Those grieving probably feel no guilt. (I didn't.) But if the grievers do feel guilty, for whatever reason, take time with them, open your Bibles, and read together. Or suggest that they talk to a pastor or biblical counselor.

11. Don't make any major decisions for at least six months. OR You can't keep up your house by yourself. (If you are thinking of giving advice to grievers, don't.)

Advice is worthless unless asked for. If you are really close to those grieving, they will probably ask for some help in sorting things out, but in their own time. At the funeral or shortly thereafter, the grievers need your encouragement and support, not your advice.

12. You just have to get over it yourself. (Please do not say this.)

Just think how cold this sounds. The person saying this must not understand the power and strength of God. His love, mercy, and grace. Talk to the grievers about God, about how through His Word they will be able to get through this most difficult time. Remind them that God is the Great Healer. Tell the griever you want to be with them; that you love them; that they are special to you. Let the grievers know they can call on you anytime.

13. <u>At least he isn't suffering anymore.</u>

Realize that, to those grieving, this isn't as comforting as you might think it would be. Say the departed ones are with the Lord; that they were saved, are rejoicing with the angels, and are walking with Jesus. These things are very comforting to those grieving.

Needed a Christian Sister

Please, Christian Sister, come along beside me. Lead me to God's Word. Don't just tell me what to read, sit down with me. Let's read and discuss what the verse(s) teach. I know it's easiest for you to suggest I read such and such a chapter or verse; please don't leave it at that.

Come visit me. Sit with me. Pray with me. Cry with me. Laugh with me. Open our Bibles and read with me or maybe read to me. Teach me God's Word. Even if I already know that verse, explain it to me. Help me to apply it right now. For, you see, my mind is not very clear and I'm having trouble concentrating when I'm alone.

Remind me of the truth of God's Word. I know it, but I need to hear it again. Help me to focus on God, not myself.

Comfort me with words of hope. Even though I grieve the loss of Bud, I still have the hope of being reunited with him in heaven. He was saved. Let us read together:

Brothers, we do not want you to be ignorant, about those who fall asleep, or grieve like the rest of men, who have no hope.

(1 Thessalonians 4:13)

It would be so nice to just sit with someone who genuinely wants to try to understand my feelings, my thoughts, and my desires. Encourage me to just hang on and let God do the rest. Remind me that in time God will bring about the renewing and healing of my heart. I can lean on Him always.

Then your light will break forth like dawn, and your healing will quickly appear.

(Isaiah 58:8a)

He heals the brokenhearted and binds up their wounds.

(Psalm 147:3)

Part III

Grieving Journey

O Lord . . . if you will, please grant success to the journey on which I have come.

(Genesis 24:42b)

The Past Again

The past! Will the past ever be the past? Will I ever stop thinking about the past? When will I leave the past in the past?

I am intent on remembering the sadness and pain. I'm desperately clinging to every hurt and negative thought I've ever had. I've balanced myself on a high, high branch, and I'm ready to fall. I'm hanging on as tight as I can, because if I fall, it will end the pain and right now I am not seeking relief. I just let those thoughts keep coming, one after another.

Soon I will be out of thoughts and out of my mind.

These thoughts are frightening to me.

Suddenly my thoughts are shifting again. Somewhere down deep, I realize that if I am to find peace and joy in the future, I must overcome my difficult past and my present state of mind.

Journey Begins

As I start out, I am sure this journey will be a rigorous, emotionally draining trip. I will be taking the low road, even though it will be the most difficult and treacherous to follow. A challenge I must overcome.

The road is extremely narrow, with steep hills and deep valleys. The climb is bound to deplete my energy. It will get lonely. It will get slippery, with ice on the narrow passages. I must be careful of potholes, just waiting for a missed step. Posted detour signs, not to be followed, lest I lose my way.

I am uncertain and fearful. I am carrying a bag full of junk, hoping to empty it along the way.

Come with me now, on my reflective journey through grief. When grief has settled on me like a thick, mucky fog.

Seasons of Life

$\mathcal{I}$ call to mind Scripture, Ecclesiastes specifically:

> There is a time for everything,
> and a season for everything under heaven:
> a time to be born and a time to die,
> a time to plant and a time to uproot,
> a time to kill and a time to heal,
> a time to tear down and a time to build,
> a time to weep and a time to laugh,
> a time to mourn and a time to dance,
> a time to scatter stones and a time to gather them,
> a time to embrace and a time to refrain,
> a time to search and a time to give up,
> a time to keep and a time to throw away,
> a time to tear and a time to mend,
> a time to be silent and a time to speak,
> a time to love and a time to hate,
> a time for war and a time for peace.
> (Ecclesiastes 3:1-8)

Solomon wrote these words as he was looking back on his life. I think about the seasons of my life. I realize I have already passed through some seasons; one I am experiencing now and one which is yet to come.

Seasons of My Life

𝓛 organize the seasons of my life:

Birth to Babyhood

Childhood to Young Adulthood

Nursing School to Marriage

Married Couple to Family with Children

Career to Retirement

Husband's Death to Widowhood

Death to Heaven

Throughout each season, there was uncertainty and insecurity at times. Still, I knew God was with me, guiding and directing. I knew each season came in His time and in His way. And he has promised to be with me in my season of death.

And surely I am with you always, to the very end of the age.

(Matthew 28:20b)

Blessings

Bud passed away on August 15, 2008. On August 21, I wrote these blessings in my journal:

1. God blessed me in so many ways during the last six weeks.
2. He provided for me spiritually and brought people into my life when I needed them.
3. He watched over me each day and night.
4. He gave me strength and endurance.
5. He gave me caring and loving family and friends.
6. He gave me a wonderful church family.
7. He forgave me the one night when I had selfish thoughts, thinking only of myself.
8. He helped me to grow spiritually.
9. He called Bud, and Bud answered and was saved.
10. He provided safe travel for all.
11. He reunited our family.
12. He reconciled Bud's extended family with me.
13. His timing was perfect every time and in every incidence.
14. He gave me peace and contentment.
15. He never left me throughout Bud's illness.
16. He carried Bud's medical problems for me.
17. He gave me time to say good-bye.
18. He gave Bud peace his last two days—from physical agitation, restlessness, and pain. Which also gave me peace.
19. He led me to pray with Bud each night, and over the past two years, gave Bud the ears to hear.
20. He showed me the power of forgiveness and gave me opportunities to forgive.
21. He showed me the need to let go of caring for everyone, helping me learn to let others take care of me for a little while.

22. He gave me quiet time each day and led me to the Scriptures I needed.

Pray continually; give thanks in all circumstances, for this is God's will for you in Christ Jesus.

(1 Thessalonians 5:17-18)

Father, always keep me thankful for Your blessings and show me ways to pass blessings on to others.

My Blessing

*I*t was difficult to meet all the demands put upon me; many sacrifices had to be made.

However, my life was filled with treasures from God.

One person even told me she felt sorry for me because I had to take care of Bud.

People implied Bud was a burden to me. Caring for him did take a great deal of my time and my strength.

There were nights of lost sleep and many skipped meals. But I counted it a blessing and a privilege. God had given me an opportunity to minister to Bud and to also serve Him, my Beloved Lord. Not everyone is given that privilege.

Serve wholeheartedly, as if you were serving the Lord, not men.

(Ephesians 6:7)

Alone

August 20, 2008

This morning as I close the door, having said good-bye to Bud's cousins from Illinois, I suddenly realize: I am alone. A deep, deep dread comes into my heart. I am totally, completely alone. For the first time in my life, I will be living by myself.

I go to the couch, where Bud had slept for so many months, and I lie down and cry. I cry till I am exhausted and fall into a restless sleep. I awake; I wish I had gained some peace and wisdom in my sleep. But I know that is not how wisdom is acquired. I am just trying to fool myself, because at this moment, I am not seeking wisdom. I want relief from this pain.

I am hurting so much. My mind goes back to my comfort verse:

Casting all your care upon him; for he careth for you.
(1 Peter 5:7 [King James Study Bible])

I find my comfort in that verse, just as I always have. I know I can find peace throughout this day as I cast my cares upon God.

Sleep without Fear

Note on Piece of Paper:

This will be my first night alone without Bud or any company. I wonder if I'll be afraid. I might be, but I don't think so. I need to feel the presence of Bud. I'll sleep on the couch where Bud slept for so many nights. I tell myself it is only for tonight. I want to find comfort here, so sleep will come quickly.

Sleep does not come. Memories engulf me, like a raging river engulfs all in its path. My mind is flooded, and I feel myself drowning, going deeper and deeper under the weight of my thoughts and memories. I know now, I must go into our bed (my bed); I must find my peace and restfulness with God. God is the only One I can truly trust, and He will never leave me. He will be my ever-present companion. I recall once hearing, "When all I have is God, I have all I need."

As I cover my head, I pray and ask God to cover me with his wings for protection and grant me a night of rest. I ask Jesus to come and sit by me. In the morning I awake, rested from a good night's sleep.

I will lie down and sleep in peace,
for you alone, O LORD,
make me dwell in safety.
(Psalm 4:8)

[AUTHOR'S NOTE: *From that night till the present, I have prayed this same prayer. God blesses me every night with restful hours of sleep.*]

Advertisement

August 22, 2008

Help Wanted

Someone willing to sit and listen to me.

Someone to invite me to come out of my house and spend time with him or her.

Someone to encourage me, to comfort me.

Someone to tell me he or she loves me.

Someone to cry with me.

Someone to give me hope about the future.

Someone to read and study Scriptures with me.

Someone to just tell me I am okay.

Someone to pray with me.

Someone to help me with all my tasks.

I need help because now I have the sad task of sorting through all of Bud's things. To decide what to do with his things. I feel that if I get rid of his stuff, I am getting rid of Bud. It's an emotion I can't deal with. I need to take care of all the equipment in the yard and get the garage cleaned out. There are hundreds of other tasks to do.

I know if I allow myself to just stay in my house, remain alone and lonely, I'll grow old too soon and I will never leave. But I have no desire to leave. There is nowhere I want to go.

No one has visited me. I know only a week has passed. It has been a very, very long and lonely week. I haven't had a reason (or the energy) to even clean my house.

I'm discouraged, lonesome, and weary. I fear I'm going crazy.

Bud Is Gone

August 2008

*B*ud is gone! I can't believe it. Now what? I feel like I am suspended between not caring at all and caring too much. Both feelings are stressful, and I'm anxious. If I don't care at all, I may as well just give up right now. Yet, if I start to care too much again, I'll just get hurt again. I'm so discouraged.

Will I ever be okay again—emotionally, mentally, and spiritually? If only my brain would start to function, I could do what I need to do.

I know down deep that this is the spiritual renewal I need. But I am so exhausted and tired. I haven't even read my Bible or my devotionals since Bud died. I know it has only been a week. But I want and need to get back with God once more. Please help me, Holy Spirit.

My Life Now

I wonder what my life will be like now, with Bud gone. What will I do, and how will I manage my time? What will it be like without a hospital bed or commode in the living room? All the furniture shoved together. No oxygen condenser, noisily operating twenty-four hours a day. No tray of medication on the kitchen table.

How will I use my time? No medication to set up and administer. No nebulizer treatments twice a day. No special requests for food to prepare. No one to bathe and shave. No physical assessment needed each day. No one needing complete care. No one needing me.

How will I feel each day as I look upon the empty couch where Bud used to sleep? Or as I sit in the family room alone on the couch where we used to watch TV every night? With no one to sit beside me, no one to put his feet in my lap. To hold my hand. No one to call out to me in the middle of the night when a leg cramp needed to be massaged till relief came. No one needing pain medication, wanting me to sit with him until it took effect and he could sleep again. No one to tell me memories of his childhood in Illinois. And of his adventures in the Navy, of his travels and the things he saw.

No one to buy groceries for, even when he only wanted V8 juice, tomatoes, oranges, and Sprite. No one to take to doctor's appointments, to the lab for blood work, to the emergency room, etc. No one needing me to sit with him while he was in the hospital.

No one needing me to help fix his tractor or truck.

No one to love me, to hug me, to kiss me, or to reach out to me, even just to touch my arm.

Lonely, that's how I feel.

I'm asking You, God, "What will my life be like now without Bud?" Please, God, help me feel joy, peace, and contentment once again. You are the only One who can help me.

Sunday before Church

August 24, 2008

*U*p early as usual. Today is Sunday. Your day, my Lord.

> "Observe the Sabbath day by keeping it holy, as the LORD
> your God has commanded you."
> (Deuteronomy 5:12)

I know this is your day.

> This is the day the LORD has made; let us rejoice and be
> glad in it.
> (Psalm 118:24)

I truly would like to rejoice today. Sunday used to be the best day of the week—my favorite day. My time to worship you, my Lord. To be with other believers . . . an uplifting and joyful day. A time for me to grow spiritually through Sunday school and Pastor's message.

But this morning, Father, I am dreading it. My first time at church since Bud's funeral. I know you are with me: "Take my hand, precious Lord."

> "Do not fear, for I am with you;
> do not be dismayed, for I am your God. I will
> strengthen you and help you; I will uphold you
> with my righteous right hand."
> (Isaiah 41:10)

An Invisible Person

August 25, 2008

I could barely keep from crying at church yesterday. Except for a couple of people, no one took time to even say "hi" to me. Several asked how I was doing as they walked past me.

I really don't know what I expected; I guess someone to just acknowledge that Bud was gone, or maybe ask if I wanted to talk. I just expected something, I suppose, even if I don't know exactly what. I guess it isn't fair to criticize them, because I myself don't know what I want.

Really, I would just like to say to them, "Please listen to me." But I will never say that to anyone. I want them to take the first step; I want them to ask me if I would like to talk with them. I realize they all have families to go home to.

I should consider their needs, not mine.

Understand Me

Please don't judge me or try to figure out what's going on with me. I'm having trouble figuring things out. My emotions are on a whirling roller coaster. I'm up, and then I'm down, and then I'm even sideways at times.

No one seems to care how I feel. Even at church when someone asks me, "How are you doing?" I know they want me to say "okay," so I do. They reply "that's good." They turn away, and I'm left alone to watch them talk and laugh with others.

I want to scream, "Do you not realize that I am only pretending when I'm with you? I don't want to make you feel uncomfortable." I will go home to cry. I will do all my crying in the solitude of my home, by myself, without anyone.

At Grave—First Time

August 25, 2008, Morning

At Bud's grave, I'm alone with my memories. Suddenly a lonely, dark sadness covers me like a heavy black blanket. My mind is in shock. I'm trying desperately to absorb the reality of Bud's death. I just can't. I sit on the ground, unable to stand with this weight on my back. I cry, but nothing takes away the hurt.

The Lord gave, and the Lord took away. This just keeps playing in my mind over and over, like an old-fashioned record in a jukebox. God, down deep I know it was Your will. When You took Bud, it was time. *Your time.*

Evening

Forgive me, Father, but this morning as I looked upon the ground and visualized Bud's body covered in dirt, I just couldn't find the words I needed to say to You. The words You deserve, and the words of praise You desire. They are in my heart; they just won't come out of my mouth.

Your healing powers are with me. And I know the day will come when I will speak the words of praise and worship that You deserve and desire. I just can't today.

You saved Bud, and I know he is with You now, blessed Lord and Savior.

It is Your forgiveness that I need, and I know my thoughts are sinful. I'm searching and searching to find the words to say. They just aren't coming to mind.

Coming Home

Ramblings on Piece of Paper (No Date)

I may have been gone a few minutes or a couple of hours; it didn't matter. As I drove up the hill to our house, I would feel a knot form in my stomach, my heartbeat would quicken, and my hands would shake.

I would begin to wonder what I would find when I got in the house. Had Bud fallen? Was he on the floor, unable to get up? Was he hurt? Was he sick? Was he angry? Did he need something that he couldn't get while I was gone? Or was he doing okay?

The first words I would hear as I closed the door were, "Are you home?"

Hesitating, I would say, "Yes, I'm home." I knew several requests would follow. Bring me this or that; do this or that. And many times, "I've messed up the TV again."

But then everything changed!

Now as I drive up the hill, the knot is still in my stomach, my heart still quickens, and my hands still shake. But it's not because I fear what awaits me; it's because I know *nothing* awaits me—except silence.

As I close the door, no one calls out to me. No one needs me. There is no one to care for. There is no one to talk to.

It's just me, alone with my thoughts.

Sometimes I call out, "Honey, I'm home!" I do it just to hear a voice.

Talk about Bud

August 2008

Please let me talk about Bud and our life together. Let me tell you what Bud was like when we first were married; let me talk about our life together. Lay aside your opinion and/or thoughts of Bud, unless they are uplifting to me and positive regarding Bud.

Tell me you miss Bud too. And tell me about your adventures and times spent with Bud. Let's laugh together and maybe even cry a little. Don't leave me with thoughts that Bud meant nothing to any of you. You all knew him, and some of you had a relationship with him before he and I married. Tell me about those experiences.

When I'm talking about Bud, let me relate anything and everything I choose. Just sit quietly and listen. Don't interrupt with your memories of your spouse—his or her thoughtfulness, the love you shared, and your wonderful marriage. I don't need to be reminded of how hard it will be to be alone or of how much I am going to hate it.

I am not intentionally being selfish and self-centered right now. I'm just hurting. And I am trying desperately to hang on to Bud. Memories are all I have left.

Summer Is Gone

August 2008

The weather tells me it's summer. Summer is a time for everything to be growing, to be spreading new seeds, assuring there will be new life next year.

Bud died last week. Yet the sky is still blue, and the sun still sends down its light and heat. Plants continue to grow and to produce fruits and vegetables. My flowers are blooming, putting on a magnificent display of colors. The birds are singing in concert, vocalizing and harmonizing with trills, croons, twitters, chirps, peeps, and squawks. Together, they create a melodious, pleasing sound.

I am surrounded by God's wonderful, warm, inviting creation. Yet I am frozen, cold and chilled to the bone. All I see are lakes frozen with ice. Ice storms mangling and smashing everything in sight.

Bud, my "Summers," is gone.

Falling Apart

September 2008

Up at 5:00 a.m. Now what to do with today? I am so weary, so sad, so filled with pain, so lonely, so frustrated, so discouraged, so weakened, so exhausted, so empty, and so tired of pretending that everything, including me, is okay. I am hurting so deeply, and it never ends. I should call Wanda, but I can't even reach out to a biblical friend. I keep so much inside me, and I haven't been reaching out to God. In fact, I feel like I've separated myself from Him. My only source of life and help.

As I pace the floor, my thoughts are confused, irrational, senseless, and illogical, and now I know what despondency feels like. But even in this terrible state of mind, I am not questioning You, God. I am not asking You, why?

Deep inside, I do know this is Your will. But I just can't keep my mind focused on You. Help me, please.

I sit for a few minutes, and then I walk into Bud's and my bedroom. A wave of loneliness consumes me; it is overwhelming. I am shaking, my heart is racing, and my head is pounding. I fall on the floor and call out to God to help me. "God I need You," I cry. "I am completely broken and in need of repair. I know only You can fix me, if You are still willing to do so, God."

I fall asleep on the floor.

When I awake the clock reads 11:00 a.m.; I slept for more than four hours. A sense of peace covers me, and I feel the presence of God. I know God that You are with me once more, and I am placing my trust in You.

Hear my voice when I call, O LORD;
be merciful to me and answer me. My heart says of you,
"Seek his face!"
Your face, LORD, I will seek. Do not hide your face from me,
    do not turn your servant away in anger; you have been
my helper. Do not reject me or forsake me, O God my
Savior."

(Psalm 27:7-9)

Superwoman Mode

September 2008

This is a very difficult entry for me to share, as it reveals a part of me that I would like to keep hidden. Yet I feel it is important that you understand the depths of grief that can consume a person who loses a spouse.

I remember being in autopilot mode when Bud died; now I am in superwoman mode. I tell myself, *God has given me strength, and I am going to use it.*

Journal Entry

I continue to pray and pray, asking God for the strength to just get through one day at a time. Sometimes an hour at a time. God answers my prayer; He gives me strength. But I have no fellowship with him, no patience, no healing, no power to overcome grief or to mourn—I have only physical strength.

And I continue to go it alone without God's spiritual strength. I know I'm separating myself from God more and more each day. But I'm afraid He doesn't want to hear from me. Not true! I really know He wants to hear from me. But what do I say? The words just won't come. I remind myself, no matter what I've done or how I feel, God is always with me. Just call out to Him.

I don't call out to Him; I just keep struggling along and alone. I have a single purpose, my own agenda. Get everything taken care of: all that extra legal business, phone calls, appointments, bills, etc. There is just too much to think about and too much to do. But I do it all—with drudgery in my heart. There is a loneliness constricting my heart. And heaviness fills my heart.

When I allow myself time to think, my thoughts are on myself, how lonely I am, and how I dread my circumstances of living alone for the rest of my life. I feel so discouraged. Defeat is just one thought away. I am so sad.

It just takes too much energy to even try to change these thoughts. I've lost the battle.

Loneliness

September 2008

Sitting here all alone, I cover myself with a heavy blanket of loneliness. There is a great sense of loss deep down. Each day, I go about my tasks with a heavy heart, blinking back the ever-present tears. Each night, I bury my head in a tear-soaked pillow.

I am able to react to people, offering a smile and all the right responses. But my heart still cries out—I wish Bud was here. I have no one to have coffee with each morning. No one to share the little details of life with, moment by moment.

October 2008

I can only look back on October 2008 from memory. With only a couple of journal entries, all my writing from that time was merely lists of things to do and lists of things done.

I was in that mode of getting everything done, and personal entries were not important to me. (Probably I didn't want to look at myself, knowing and fearing what I might see.)

I worked each day until I was exhausted. I didn't want to have to think about my life.

I was so driven to get the entire yard cleaned up. Equipment, tractors, junk, and everything removed. That was my only concern, and it consumed all my time, all my thoughts, and all my energy.

I do remember evenings were the hardest. Mornings were the easiest.

I know I continued to attend church and enjoyed the messages. And the fellowship, somewhat. I was active in serving. And somehow I managed to reach out to others. I was still in that state of mind where I pretended everything was all right. I just wasn't into helping myself in a healthful, God-glorifying way.

I realize now that was the month I really separated myself more and more from God.

Looking back, I wish I had stayed close to God. To let him lead me through my grief; to allow myself time to grieve. To just admit I was grieving. That it was okay to grieve. I had built a wall so strong around me that nothing and no one could penetrate it.

Planning a Trip

October 2008

*M*anda and I have just finalized our plans for our trip to Israel next April. I can't believe I am really going to Israel. I guess, God, I am beginning to feel life again. I am really looking forward to going, to walk where Jesus walked. Just to be in Your Holy Land.

I actually have a passport, and my registration is completed. All I have to do is hang on until April.

God, I am so thankful for the many blessing you have given me. Your love and watch care, the financial provision for this trip, and a wonderful friend who encouraged me to go.

Fear

October 2008

I tell people I have no fear, that I'm okay. But I do have fear deep down inside. I fear I may never get over this time in my life. It is so difficult to explain to people. I really can't explain it to myself.

I tell myself, *It's only been a couple of months. But it feels like forever.* Yet the memories of Bud's illness and death are so fresh in my mind. I can't seem to let go of them. I cling desperately to them.

I just want to sit here and remember. But when I do, I become so sad and discouraged. My mind is like a revolving door. In goes a memory, out goes that memory, and immediately it returns. Around and around and around, until I'm so dizzy that complete exhaustion takes hold and I'm ready to collapse.

Somehow I have got to move forward. How do I do it? And when will I do it? Maybe tomorrow I will start a new life.

Loneliness Returns

November 2008

There are times when I am so lonely and overwhelmed. I try to pray, but my mind is a blank canvas, and no image will appear. I try and try, but this agonizing pain will not leave my body or my mind. The hurt is so deep inside me, my stomach aches, as if I have been punched. My eyes burn from crying thousands of tears. My hands are as cold as ice. I reach out to touch the warmth of another person, seeking a soft, gentle hand to hold mine.

But no matter how far I reach, there is no one, only more coldness. I wrap myself in a fuzzy throw, but the shivering will not stop. My teeth chatter. I try to cry out, but no sound escapes my lips.

Self-Centered

November 2008

I have really become self-centered. I want the world and everyone and everything in it to be arranged according to my life, my thoughts, and my feelings. To always meet my needs and my desires.

When they don't, I withdraw; I feel rejected, I cry, I blame others. I ask myself questions: Why doesn't anyone care? Why don't they call or visit? Why, why, why?

This way of thinking just leads to a downward spiraling. I know I must stop! Because not only is it not getting me anywhere, it is also displeasing to God. God knows my every thought, even these sinful ones.

I have a plan: I will start tomorrow. I will change my thoughts in the morning.

Ready to Explode

November 2008

I just can't keep everything inside much longer. I feel like I am going to explode. My heart is ticking like a detonator on a time bomb. Seconds tick off while my head pounds. With each heartbeat, I wait for the explosion to come.

I fall on the floor. And, like Humpty Dumpty after his fall, I am shattered into a million tiny pieces. There is nothing left, just a broken shell. All the king's horses and all the king's men couldn't put Humpty Dumpty together again; nor can they do so for me.

A Corset

November 2008

I am hurting so badly, I can't let anyone into my life. I feel I have no one who wants to be in my life. It is like I have a corset on, but it is so tight that it squeezes my breath right out of me. This feeling is so strange to me. But what is even stranger is that I'm actually glad to be miserable, glad to be away from people and away from help.

I know I need someone, but I just can't reach out. A close biblical friend called yesterday, and I told her I was doing fine. I will call her back soon.

Trying to Knit

November 2008

I need something to occupy my mind. I'm not very interested in television anymore. Maybe I'll try knitting again. Make another afghan. I'll see. It just sounds like too much work right now. My mind just isn't cooperating; it just takes off on its own path. I need a radio tower, like airplanes have, to keep my mind flying in the right direction.

December 2008

I finally got some yarn to make a baby sweater. It will be nice to have if someone has a baby. I bought blue yarn. Why? What if it's a girl? Guess I'll take the yarn back. No, I'll just keep it: the baby could be a boy. I can't continue with this internal dialogue going back and forth; I'm driving myself crazy. I'll just put the yarn away. I didn't want to knit anyway.

January 2009

I just give up. I couldn't even follow a simple stitch when I tried knitting yesterday. Why won't my mind concentrate? It is such a simple stockinet stitch, which I've done many, many times. Oh well, it really doesn't matter. I don't know anyone who is having a baby.

The Train

November 2008

I see the light of a train rapidly approaching me. The light blinds me, and I can't move. The engine hits with such quickness and force, I'm unable to get out of the way. The pain is excruciating as the wheels roll over me. The weight on my chest is so heavy, I fear I will suffocate. Lying under the huge steel engine, the darkness overcomes me. I am bruised and alone. I am completely drained of all emotions. God, this can't be Your desire for me. Please show me what You would have me do. I will do my best. I promise.

The Rapids

November 2008

I feel as if I am about to go headfirst over the raging falls. The roar of the rapids is deafening; the waves hurl me toward the falls. I'm unable to hold myself afloat. I close my eyes and wait for the increasing power of the water to push me over the falls. As I feel myself falling, I hold my breath, waiting for that sudden stop on the rocks below. I will soon be shattered into a million splinters. All hope is gone.

Thanksgiving 2008

November 5, 2008

I've decided to have Thanksgiving here this year. It will be fun to have a Thanksgiving Day like we used to. To have all the family here once again. I am not really sure I want to, but I think I need to. I just want to do normal things again. There will be about twenty people here. And I know Connie, my great-niece, will bring her baby. Babies are so precious. That will be the highlight of my day.

November 25, 2008

Two days until Thanksgiving. I pretty much have things ready. It's been a lot of work, and I'm so tired. I just can't seem to get my energy back. I'm still good at pretending, so no one will know. I wish I hadn't volunteered. I just wanted it to be like it used to be on Thanksgiving. But I realize now, things will never be the same. I can't let myself get down today. I have too much to do.

November 28, 2008

Thanksgiving is over. And I am so glad. Twenty-five people came. Connie did bring little Landon. What a cutie. But the rest of the day was horrible. I know now I'm going crazy—a little more each day. I felt like I was in the Twilight Zone. I couldn't even remember Kelsie's (great-niece) name. I covered it up, but I didn't recognize Lesli (another great-niece) either. And so many people talking at once. I wonder what I said or didn't say that I should have said. I just wanted everyone to leave. I'll not do Thanksgiving ever again. In fact, I just want to hide out in my house and not see anyone ever again.

Satan in My Life

November 2008

S atan is working not only to tear me down but also to tear me apart. He is dragging my spirit down and down into a deep well—hoping to drown it forevermore. He is using my uncontrollable thoughts to push me under the water. I'm just too tired to resist. I don't want to try anymore.

Emotions

November 2008

Without warning, another great rush of emotions floods my mind. I catch myself staring to cry. Tears are flowing, and then suddenly I feel stronger, and the sadness leaves. These emotions come and go every day. Just as waves break on the shore and then return to the ocean. My emotions come in a rush and then retreat just as quickly, leaving me exhausted and confused.

Some days I write in my journal three or four times. I feel driven to put everything on paper—emotions, thoughts, and feelings. I need to analyze each one. If I do that, maybe I can figure out how to stop the waves.

Tormenting questions swirl within my head, like a whirlwind threatening to knock my head completely off my shoulders.

What will become of me? My life? Who will help me? Does anyone care? Will anyone be there if I need something? What am I to do with the lonely years ahead? Will I ever get over this? When? Am I always going to have a broken heart? Always be confused and sad? Will my joy ever come back?

Lesson to Be Learned

December 2008

Today as I sit and think, which is about all I do anymore, I thought about when I cried out to God for help. I realize that just asking for help is not enough; nor is admitting brokenness, or confessing and repenting. It takes my commitment, time, and energy. All of which are available through the Holy Spirit. And my part, after asking, is to use them.

I am still struggling with my studying, my prayers, my daily devotions, and my daily living. I do try, but my concentration just isn't there.

Last week, a very close relationship fell apart. I'm still trying to figure that out. People do not call, and if they do, it is only infrequently. No one visits; no one seems to care. When I do see people, I have to go to them. Even church people don't seem to be concerned.

Christmas

December 26, 2008

✐eresa and the boys came yesterday for Christmas. They opened gifts, ate, and left. I know the boys had to go with their dad to his family.

I have come to realize one thing: I can't go back—back to the days of yesteryear. Christmas will never be the same. I should have learned this from Thanksgiving. I also know that I am not the same.

Although I do better at times, I was so sad yesterday. I did rejoice in the birth of Jesus. After everyone left, I read Luke, chapter 2. It is a wonderful reminder of Jesus' birth, a reminder to look ahead to when He will die on the cross for my sins. Forgive me, Father, for not reading the Christmas story to my kids this year.

A new year is approaching. I'll do better (maybe).

Failing God

January 2009

I have failed God. During this time of grieving, I have become selfish and self-centered. I tell myself I don't care and I can't help it. I wallow in self-pity, like a pig wallows in mud. And I have become just as dirty and disgusting as a pig. The more I think about myself and being alone, the muddier I get. I feel the mud cover me so completely, I can no longer move. I just lay in that muddy pool of self-loathing and self-deception.

Today, alone in the dark, a small light flickers in the darkness, as I once again pick up my Bible. I know a truth: God will never leave me or forsake me or reject me. Holy Spirit, lead me today to the Scripture I need right now.

I search my concordance, finding this:

Those who know your name will trust in you, for you,
LORD, have never forsaken those who seek you.
(Psalm 9:10)

I study and study; I read and I concentrate on God's Word. This is something that has been missing in my life. I have given up so much, wasted so much time. I bought in to the many lies of Satan. I let him lead me into that pigpen. How he must have delighted to see me rooting and rooting in the thick ugly mess that I had turned my life into. And I have disappointed my God. I know it will take time to get the mud off my body, to remove the mud from my eyes and my ears. I shed tears of remorse and regret.

And then I pray: Dear Holy God, I know Your Spirit is within me still. And you have just been waiting for me to return. I am here begging for forgiveness—for not returning sooner; for leaving you, my loving Father. Forgive me, Father, for my sins of _____.

[AUTHOR'S NOTE: *I have chosen not to include my entire prayer from that day. It is too personal. But I know God heard my confession and forgave me. And I have repented. Praise God for His mercy and grace.*]

> Then I acknowledged my sin to you
> and did not cover up my iniquity. I said, "'I will confess
>   my transgressions to the LORD"—
> and you forgave the guilt of my sin.
>   Selah
>
> (Psalm 32:5)

Weight of Grief

I see where the weight of grief continues to hamper my fellowship with my God. It keeps me underwater, where I keep my eyes closed, unable to look to Jesus.

Several anchors weigh me down: selfishness, negative attitudes, my sinful nature, and worldly cares and problems. These pull me to the bottom, where there is darkness. I can't get loose; I'm drowning. Help me, Lord, help me! I feel the release of the anchors, as if the ropes have been severed. I float to the surface, where Jesus is waiting with open arms. I feel secure.

Part IV

End of

Grieving Journey

Grieving Journey Comes to an End

As my grieving journey comes to an end, many "whys" are swirling around in my head.

Why didn't I just depend on God?
Why didn't I live by God's truths?
Why didn't I use the strength of God, which was so available?
Why didn't I look to God, instead of to myself, for hope and revival?
Why didn't I let God carry my burdens?
Why didn't I rely on God, instead of wanting other people?

Why? Why?! Why!! The "whys" go on and on and on.

The most important why: why did I wait so long to deal with my personal failures and sins?

I knew I couldn't hide from God; I couldn't pretend he didn't know. I really do not have a reasonable answer to those "whys." But I do know a truth: God was in control throughout my whole grieving journey. And when it was his time, he set my path on a marvelous spiritual journey.

I am sure I would not have grown spiritually, as I have, if I had not suffered as I did. God always knows what is best for me, and when He allows trials and suffering into my life, it is for my good.

Now come with me as I leave the darkness and move into the light.

I have come into the world as a light, so no one who believes in me should stay in darkness.

(John 12:46)

The Other Side of Grief

I thought it would never happen, but it did. I'm up early as usual, prayer said and coffee in hand. I sit silently and bow before God. I feel so different. I am at peace, not from a restful sleep, but as if the sun in its most brilliant radiance is in my heart. I feel as light as a balloon, floating up into the blue, blue sky.

I feel the presence of God, once again, smiling at me, holding out His hand as if to say, "Come, my child and walk with me. I have something special planned for you."

"Thank You, God; I really am going to make it. You are great," I whisper.

I am on the other side of grief. I know I am stronger. I've learned and gained knowledge. I know now to hang on to God's Word with all my might. To always lean on Him as He holds me close.

In the past, I didn't see the lessons God was trying to teach me. Nor did I hold tight enough to the truths and promises of God's Word. Now through God's mercy and grace, this difficult journey of grief has ended. Praise and Glory to my almighty God!

I will exalt you, my God the King;
    I will praise your name for ever and ever.
Every day I will praise you
    and extol your name for ever and ever.

Great is the LORD and most worthy of praise;
    his greatness no one can fathom.
One generation will commend your works to another;
    they will tell of your mighty acts.
They will speak of the glorious splendor of your majesty,
    and I will meditate on your wonderful works.
They will tell of the power of your awesome works,
    and I will proclaim your great deeds.

GRIEVING FOR THE GLORY OF GOD

They will celebrate your abundant goodness
and joyfully sing of your righteousness. The LORD is
gracious and compassionate,
slow to anger and rich in love.
"The LORD is good to all;
he has compassion on all he has made."
(Psalm 145:1-9)

Part V

Prologue to

Spiritual Journey

Do not conform any longer to the pattern of this world,
but be transformed by the renewing of your mind.
Then you will be able to test and approve
what God's will is—
His good, pleasing and perfect will.
(Romans 12:2)

Before Spiritual Journey

As we continue our journey, you will be filled with joy and hope. Before we start on this journey, I must go back in time a bit. I must return once more to the years of Bud's illness. For that is when my sincere and genuine walk with Jesus began.

I accepted Jesus as my Savior in March 2004. My daughter was saved in January, and she encouraged me to come to her church and learn more about Jesus. And it was there I was saved. I began to read the Bible, starting with Genesis. I found some verses difficult to read and understand. But I persevered, and I slowly gained some knowledge and understanding. I continued to attend that church.

Many things happened in 2004. A close and dear uncle died in January. My aunt required a pacemaker in February. Also in February, my daughter was married. In April, my niece's mother died unexpectedly (of acute leukemia). Sometime during the summer, close family relationships were broken. My son's house burned in November, and he came to stay with us. December ended with Bud having three stents placed in arteries in his heart. (Two arteries had 99 percent blockages, and the other had a 100% blockage.)

It was then that God intervened in my life. I learned a truth: His timing is always perfect, and He always has a perfect plan for my life.

As for God, his way is perfect;
the word of the LORD is flawless. He is a shield
for all who take refuge in him.

(Psalm 18:30)

An Invitation

There is a knock at the door. It's 7:00 p.m.; I hope it doesn't wake Bud up. A surprise: Wanda is standing there. She is as surprised as I am, because she didn't know this was my house. She is here to invite kids to AWANA at her church. Of course, I have no little kids. She then invites me to come to church. I tell her that I really have been considering it. I'll see, maybe in a couple of weeks.

Thinking back to that night, I see God was working throughout my life. Moving me in the direction He wanted me to go. Wanda and I were friends, although not close, in childhood. And throughout the years we had many occasions to get together. I was very close friends with her sister-in-law.

Now God brought Wanda and me together, and we instantly became very close friends. Later we became Christian sisters and true biblical friends. She led me through God's Word, and she became my mentor and a source of much biblical teaching. Since that time she has been an encourager and support person; an example of a godly woman. I thank God for her every day.

My First Day at a New Church

December 2004

*A*s I walk into the church, I am apprehensive, because I don't know what to expect and I don't know anyone. Wanda immediately comes to me and invites me to sit with her. I am glad she did, but she sits near the front of the church, and I am uncomfortable. I do see a couple of people I know.

I just sit and look around. I can't believe it, it's like I've entered a whole new world. (In fact, I have.) I have entered into God's house, and I am surrounded by God's family. The congregation joins in songs, prayers, and worship. Pastor preaches from the Bible and quotes Scriptures, explaining their implementation in our lives. Everyone seems happy to be here. I silently thank God for bringing me to this church.

Soon I am attending Sunday school before church. We are studying about witnessing to others. This is overwhelming to me. But I do read my book and look up the suggested Scriptures.

> But you will receive power when the Holy Spirit comes on you; and you will be my witnesses in Jerusalem, and in all Judea and Samaria, and to all the ends of the earth.
> (Acts 1:8)

I read and study other Scriptures. But I know I will be hesitant to speak out to others. I am given a little card: "Share Jesus without Fear." I put it in my purse; I will always carry it.

The Little Bible Baptist Church

A Bible teaching church is what we all need,
A pastor willing to plant a seed.

A place where people are feed,
With the word of God and his daily bread.
Where fountains of living water flows faithfully,
No darkness prevails, only a light glowing eternally.
Our church is white, with a name in bold letters,
Telling all, this is where the children of God gathers.
So come on in and see for yourself, and when you do,
You'll find a loving family welcomes you.

Meeting with Pastor

January 2005, Journal Entry

I am meeting with Pastor and his wife, Ruth, this afternoon. I am anxious and fearful. My life is such a mess. I can no longer deal with my situation and/or my circumstances. Everything that affects me is out of my control. I want to just stop trying. Things just keep getting worse. I hope Pastor can help me.

I sit down with Pastor and Ruth. As I start to talk, my hands begin to shake, and my voice quivers. I try hard not to cry, but the tears fall. I can hardly get the words out. All of a sudden, I realize Pastor and Ruth are listening intently to what I am saying. No one has ever paid that much attention to what I say. Ever!

It is difficult to fully grasp what Pastor is telling me. He says help is available, if I am willing to work hard and study God's Word on a daily basis. I say, "Yes, I am." (But I am thinking to myself, *I thought you were going to tell me what to do.*) My answer of what to do comes from Ruth. She suggests I do an individual Bible study with her. I agree. We set a day and time.

As I leave, my tears are gone, and I feel less stressed and less anxious.

Bible Study with Ruth

January 2005

I start my Bible study with Ruth. We meet once a week. On my own, I read through the Bible once again.

I devour all the books Ruth gives me to read. I study very hard and do all my assignments. I began to understand the Scriptures Ruth assigns to me. Ruth puts a lot of emphasis on memorization. I find it very difficult, but I do it. The first verse she has me memorize is from Corinthians:

No temptation has seized you except what is common to man. And God is faithful; he will not let you be tempted beyond what you can bear. But when you are tempted, he will also provide a way out so that you can stand up under it.

(1 Corinthians 10:13)

My Bible study continues for about three months.

I attend church and Sunday school regularly. I am intent on learning all that I can. I want to have knowledge of Scripture and be able to apply it to my life. Pastor stresses the importance of context, context. So I always try to read related verses.

God is leading me, providing many new opportunities to learn, to help others, and to serve my church.

Wanda guides and helps me as I begin serving at church. She encourages and supports me, and I take on new responsibilities.

Baptism and Membership in the Church

April 2005

*F*ollowing Jesus' example, I am baptized. What an uplifting and joyful day! Many of my family and friends are able to attend. Wanda once told me that baptism is an outward sign of my inward faith.

Peter replied, "Repent and be baptized every one of you, in the name of Jesus Christ for the forgiveness of your sins."
(Acts 2:38a)

We were therefore buried with him through baptism into death in order that, just as Christ was raised from the dead through the glory of the Father, we too may have a new life.
(Romans 6:4)

Baptism also identifies me with Christ and with the community of believers. That day I also joined the Bible Baptist Church in Augusta.

So in Christ we who are many from one body, and each member belongs to all the others.
(Romans 12:5)

Part VI

Spiritual Journey

*Go in peace.
Your journey has the LORD's approval.*
(Judges 18:6b)

It's All About God

I am taking my first step in returning to God's Word and gaining spiritual maturity.

I'm so excited, mainly because I know the ending from the beginning of this spiritual journey; I also know the middle:

The beginning starts with anticipation of what is to come.

The middle is where the hard work is done.

The ending results in a transformed me, when I am healed and return to God.

The middle will be exhausting at times, because that is where I must take responsibility for my past actions and for the future.

Do not merely listen to the word, and so deceive yourselves.
Do what it says.

(James 1:22)

The day Bud died, I know God was with me. It was I who separated myself from Him; how I wallowed in self-pity and became self-centered.

I did not concentrate on the One who is in the business of transformation. I know with the help of the Holy Spirit, I will be able to describe how God transformed me and made me whole once more.

I am continually growing spiritually.

I pray as you read my spiritual journey you will see God's Glory and Holiness.

Ascribe to the LORD the glory due his name; worship the LORD in the splendor of his holiness.

(Psalm 29:2)

Listen to God

*I*t was like God was telling me, "You want me to make it as if Bud had not died. I won't do that, but I will help you to change, for you have humbly returned to me. If you are willing, we will start today. I will guide you along the path you started a long time ago. You can once again live in harmony with me."

And that you may love the LORD your God, listen to his voice, and hold fast to him.

(Deuteronomy 30:20a)

I want to listen to God; I want to let His voice lead me. I must also read and study His Word.

This is what we speak, not in words taught us by human wisdom but in words taught by the Spirit, expressing spiritual truths in spiritual words.

(1 Corinthians 2:13)

Yes, Lord, I have been taught Your spiritual words and truths. I am now returning to them—and to You—once again.

Start of Spiritual Journey

I am delighted that you have continued with me thus far. As I continue my journey, you will be amazed how God has filled me with joy and hope. You will see my road become safe, secure, straight, and well maintained. There will be a bright light guiding the way as I climb upward toward the top.

The trip up to now has been rigorous, just as I expected it would be. I fell into a few potholes, but I missed a few also. At times the detour signs fooled me and lead me astray. Ice caused me to slip and even fall now and then. But now I am ready to continue: my junk bag has collected some trash and will continue to collect even more. My huge spiritual bag is already starting to collect the promises of God, and my healing has started.

"But for you who revere my name, the sun of righteousness will rise with healing in its wings. And you will go out and leap like calves released from the stall."

(Malachi 4:2a)

I expected my grieving journey to be liked a mile run, but it turned out to be a marathon. And now I know my spiritual journey shall be an even longer marathon. It will not end until my final journey begins. That final journey will begin when Jesus calls me home and I join Dad in heaven. What a glorious time that will be. And it will be forever and forever.

I am so eager to begin this jubilant and uplifting spiritual journey, and I am happy to have you along. Welcome!

Depths of Depression

November 2008

God, I thought I was doing so much better. But this morning, I have fallen into the depths of depression once more. I cried most of the night. Despair floats over me like a soft summer breeze sweeps over a meadow. In a way it is comforting to me. I don't have to move or do anything. I can just lay here and enjoy the breeze as it swirls over me.

Invitation for Counseling

November 2008, the Sabbath

This morning, God, I'm asking you to just show me a way to get myself together, so I don't have to pretend any longer. I want to use your strength and power. I know that, at times, my thoughts and attitude have not been pleasing to you. I really want to change.

I've read Your Scriptures and books on changing attitudes and thoughts. I just haven't been able to put all that knowledge into practice. (Now I'm wondering if I just didn't want to.)

I know, dear Lord, I have been disobedient to You. And this is just causing me to spiral downward more and more, deeper and deeper into depression.

Please, Father, help me.

The Next Day

Yesterday was a special day for me, God. You are so great. You heard my prayer and answered it. Praise and thanks to You, my Lord.

Yesterday, before Pastor gave his message, Katie spoke to us (and I felt she was talking directly to me). She was seeking people to counsel, biblically. She needed a certain number of supervised counseling hours to be certified as an NANC counselor. (This Katie is not my cousin.) After church, I told Katie I was interested in her counseling. And that what I wanted through the counseling was to grieve in a way that would bring glory to God.

We set a date and time to start.

First Counseling Session

November 15, 2008

Katie is coming tonight. I'm really kind of excited. I hope she can help me. You know, God, I really don't like how I've been acting; I don't like these thoughts that just won't go away. I try to rationalize (now there is a word from the past), but I can't make everything okay. Enough! My mind will be open to whatever Katie has to say. Thank You, Father, for this opportunity to get back on track. See, it's working already—I'm once again including you in my writing. Time to go. I must clean my house.

November 16, 2008

Last night was a lot different than I expected. Katie explained about biblical counseling. I know it's really going to help me. But there will be a lot of homework, which I didn't expect. Guess my mind will be tested and put to work. Katie is great and very understanding. She really knows a lot about the Bible. Another surprise: she tapes our sessions for her supervisor. That really doesn't bother me. My life is what it is. A mess! I'm going to start this morning on my first assignment. I have to write about what makes Bud's homegoing so difficult for me. Katie may get more information than she expected.

First Homework Assignment

Write about what makes the homegoing of Bud so difficult.

Actual Writing

I had time to talk with Bud and said a lot of things. Among them: "We had a good marriage"; "I love you, and I always have"; "Good-bye, I'll see you in heaven." There were countless other things I got to say throughout his illness.

Since he's been gone, there are so many things I wish I had said. Especially recalling the good times we had. Just the memories we made.

I knew the end was near, but I really didn't believe it. He always got better no matter how ill he was.

After he died, I realized I was going to be living alone for the first time in my life. From the very first day, I've had no fear of being alone. God protects me. What hurts is not having Bud with me; not having someone to care for, someone to talk with. I want someone to sit next to me on the couch in the evening. I have no one to give me hugs and kiss me good night. I'm lonely.

I'm lost as to what I should do or not do. (Not about business stuff, taking care of the house, etc.) What am I supposed to do about me? I pretend a lot that I'm okay.

I don't question God as to why He took Bud. I just question what I am going to do to now.

My Thoughts

I don't know what to do with this overwhelming sadness.

I want to talk about Bud and my memories, but no one wants to listen or respond. I've told this to several people who knew Bud for many years. Yet they do not offer any memories, or they just change the subject.

Not everything is difficult. Today I see the blessings in the Lord's calling him home. I know he is rejoicing in heaven right now.

I didn't think I was angry, but I think I am. Not at God. I'm joyous and at peace knowing God saved him and called him home.

Really it's not so much that I'm angry, it's just my life is so different. I really don't think I even have the energy to be angry. I feel like I'm stumbling in the dark all the time. Things that were routine are now a tremendous task. Although I've always been responsible for all household things, Bud made decisions regarding things I didn't know about: the car, major repairs, mechanical things, etc. The other decisions we made together. Now no matter how small or large a decision, I must make it now. Alone. I have focused a lot of time and energy on "getting things done."

I know many spiritual truths. I trust and have complete faith in God. Yet I struggle to apply these truths to everyday living. Before Bud passed away, I could read, understand, and apply God's Word. I can relate incidences of God being with me continually in the past. He is with me even now.

I know I stumble and I fall. It's so difficult to pick myself up again. Yes, I do ask God to help, and He does. Sometimes I don't ask.

Vacation with God

November 27, 2008

I am so excited I am going on a vacation with God. This vacation is also a physical, earthly vacation with Butch and Nancy. Although hesitant, I said I would go. Everyone said that it would be good for me and I deserve it (a worldly view). I said I wanted to spend time alone to get my head on straight.

Thinking about it, I realize what I need is revival, renewal, and regeneration of my soul and heart. I want to focus on God and become closer to him.

So this morning, as I'm finishing my preparations for my trip, I am thanking God for this opportunity to go to Florida. I am seeking healing, appropriate grieving, learning God's Word, fun, and relaxation—and to do it all God's way.

Here is my prayer:

Dear Heavenly Holy Father,

Thank You for giving me this opportunity to come closer and closer to you. I am asking that You give me concentration and the ability to retain what I read and learn. That I will understand and apply Your Word. That my mind will stay alert and I will be able to memorize Your Word. Give me the motivation and desire to spend my time in Your Word and with You. I need Your help and strength. Help me to see any secret sins I have hidden in my heart. Put me on the path to righteousness once more.

In Jesus' precious name I pray.
Amen.

November 28, 2008

We arrive safely in Florida after spending the night in Nashville. The long car ride each day gives me a lot of time to focus and concentrate on God. I do this from memory as I have trouble reading in the car.

As we travel, I see God as the divine Creator that He is. The magnificent colors of the trees as they are changing from green to multicolored. The sight of massive mountains rising up out of the ground, as if they are growing. The indescribable, awe-inspiring scenery. As each mile passes, the terrain seems to take on a different appearance: hilly, flat, treed, barren, rocky, river-run, dry, colorful, foggy, misty, rainy, sunlit. The most beautiful of all are the sunrises and sunsets.

I feel God's presence as I talk silently to him much of the time. Often my thoughts are disconnected, and my mind wanders. Each time, I ask God to help me get my thoughts in line with His Word. My thoughts are too numerous to write down. The underlying theme, though, is "me." I seek healing and comfort. However, I have not owned up to my part: trust and faith in the Lord. Deep down inside I have wanted God to perform a miracle, and then boom, He would say, "There, Connie, you are healed, and everything in your life is perfect."

I am able to refocus, and with humility, I ask God to forgive my selfishness and give me the wisdom I need.

November 29, 2008

We are on our way to Mobile, Alabama, to visit Butch's step-grandson and his wife. We are meeting them at a memorial for the USS *Alabama*, a battleship. As we travel along, a thought crosses my mind: I can take pictures of the ship and show Bud. (Bud was stationed on the USS *St. Paul*.) Immediately I stop that thought, but I am not sad. I thank God that Bud's memory is still with me. Bud told me about his time in the Navy and the many adventures he had. I only wish I listened more closely. All the way there, the memories just continue to flow into my mind.

When I first see the ship, I just stand and stare. It is more than huge, it is enormous: five stories up and five stories down. Nancy and

I tour the ship together. As we go through the ship, seeing the different areas, I tell Nancy what Bud told me about his ship. Nancy listens attentively. It is so joyful, like having Bud talking to me.

God, I thank You for giving me this opportunity to feel close to Bud and for having Nancy to quietly listen to me. A great day!

Earthquake

December 2008

I feel as if an earthquake has hit my life. My relationship with someone very dear and close has shifted, knocking me off balance. I feel like everything is out of my control; it came so unexpectedly. I stumble from the shock and disappointment of it all. I cry, trying not to respond to the aftershock of this earthquake.

I know God is in control, and I trust Him. But I am not sure my heart will recover from this.

A few days later, Katie comes for my biblical counseling session. We talk about my situation. The terrible thoughts and feelings I have. I feel like I've taken a tremendous fall; forgetting God's faithfulness and love.

She reminds me I need to look to Jesus' suffering and His resurrection. To seek Jesus, He will lift me up, no matter how far down I am. I can be an overcomer, just as Jesus was, as I face this difficult situation.

And my joyful obedience to God can be an encouraging example to others.

We look up Scripture, finding this:

> And being found in appearance as a man, he humbled himself and became obedient to death—even death on a cross!
> (Philippians 2:8)

Lesson

Jesus was fully man. Though Jesus is God, He humbled himself and became a man. Jesus suffered on the cross, a most cruel form of death.

He was perfect, yet He humbled himself and died as a criminal. He did this out of obedience to His Father and to carry out His Father's plan for salvation for all people who believe.

As Katie and I talk, I learn: I can face any difficulty, expected or unexpected, because my God, who is faithful, is always in control. She explains a new technique to me. The technique of put off/put on. In God's Word I am commanded to put aside sinful practices of my old self. Through God's Word I will change by putting on Christlike practices. All I need to do is spend time in God's Word each day, and then be obedient to his commands.

You were taught, with regard to your former way of life, to put off your old self, which is being corrupted by its deceitful desires; to be made new in the attitude of your minds, and to put on the new self, created to be like God in true righteousness and holiness.

(Ephesians 4:22-24)

Katie and I talk about this Scripture and how I can apply it to my life each day. I need to put off everything from my past that is harmful to me: sinful thoughts, attitudes, desires, and behaviors. And then I need to put on a new way of thinking that comes from knowing God and His Word. The Holy Spirit will lead me in the right direction. Katie gives me my homework assignment: to look up additional Scriptures, and to write out which behaviors, attitudes, and thoughts I need to put off and which I need to put on. I always do my assignments.

Homework

Put Off	Put On
Negative thoughts of rejection	Thoughts that are pleasing to God
I want to stay away from ———	I plan to visit ——— often
Stop thinking about myself	Find ways to help and love ———
Stop being disobedient to God's Word	Start being obedient to God
	Look up additional Scriptures on obedience

Therefore everyone who hears these words of mine and puts them into practice is like a wise man who built his house on the rock.

(Matthew 7:24a)

Lesson

I am to build my life on Jesus and God's Word. I am to be obedient to God's will, regardless of my situation.

Give me understanding, and I will keep your law and obey it with all my heart.

(Psalm 119:34)

Lesson

It is very important to understand what God's Word says so that I can apply it to my life by being obedient.

This is love for God: to obey his commands. And his commands are not burdensome.

(1 John 5:3)

Lesson

I want to do God's will for my life, not my will. As I pray for guidance, I will trust in the Lord, for I know He has the power to give that guidance. I will let the Holy Spirit lead; He will place me on firm solid ground and on the path of righteousness.

Teach me to do your will, for you are my God; may your good spirit lead me to level ground.

(Psalm 143:10)

Applications

1. What do you need to put off today? Negative thoughts? Sinful behaviors? Negative attitude?

2. What do you need to put on today? Be specific. Where will you learn God's Word, which will lead to obedience? Will you make a specific schedule indicating time and place?

3. How much time and energy are you willing to invest, each day, to find help in God's Word?

4. Are you willing to try the put off/put on technique?

Christmas Is Coming

December 2008

I'm dreading Christmas, and yet joyfully anticipating it. I'm still having conflicting emotions within myself.

Thanksgiving was such a disappointment. I just wasn't myself, and the holiday was such a letdown. No need to think about that all over again; I wrote about in a November journal entry. And I have prayed and talked with God about my thoughts and attitude.

Now I must concentrate on Christmas. I want to make it a joyous occasion for Teresa and the boys.

Sheri, Shirley's daughter-in-law, sent me four booklets about grieving, written by Kenneth C. Hauck. In one of the booklets he suggested that grieving persons find a way to connect their beloved spouses with people who were in their life.

I have decided to buy a special Christmas gift for a few people.

Teresa (daughter): a squirrel ornament (Bud called her "squirrel," when she was little.)

Terry Lee (grandson): one of his PaPPaw's quilted flannel shirts, with candy in the pocket (Bud always hid candy in his shirt pocket, and when Terry Lee was little he would climb in his lap to get the candy).

Tanner (grandson): a pair of socks (PaPPaw was always telling him to put on stockings or his feet would freeze).

Scott (son): a new shirt (Bud wanted Scott to dress warmly, regardless of the weather).

Butch and Nancy (brother and sister-in-law): a book about dogs (they had a dog, Duke; Bud was very fond of Duke).

Katie (cousin): a pretty dish (Bud always commented on her dishes when we ate at her house).

Bill (cousin; Katie's husband): an old bobber of Bud's (a reminder of a joke from long, long ago).

Shirley (cousin): card stock (Bud enjoyed her homemade cards, which she often sent him); a bag of beans (Bud always said, "No one makes baked beans like Shirley.").

Susan (niece): a book about dogs (Bud always worried that she had too many dogs to care for).

Laura (great-niece): a sheep ornament (Bud let her ride my sheep when she was little).

Ellie (great-great-niece): a box of chocolate candy and a box of Band-Aids (Bud always gave her chocolate candy, and she was very concerned when she saw a Band-Aid on Uncle Bud's "owie"; she was three years old at that time).

A Biblical Friend

January 2009

A biblical friend is at the door. I really don't want company today. She stays anyway. I am gracious and make coffee.

I try to hide my hurt, but she sees it on my face and in my posture. Gently she suggests some Scriptures, as she did so often when Bud was ill.

She tells me my emotions are real, but they will change as I read and learn more about God's Word. She also reminds me that Jesus wept. If Jesus, who was perfect, cried when he was sad, I know it is okay for me to cry. What comfort this brings to me.

Jesus wept.

(John 11:35)

Before she leaves, she says a prayer with me and for me. I see why and how it is so helpful to have a biblical friend. This friend listens as I talk about my feelings, my emotions, and Bud. And then she leads me to seek God's Word and to pray.

Rejoice with those who rejoice; mourn with those who mourn.

(Romans 12:15)

No matter what my situation may be, I need to be sensitive and compassionate to the problems, hardships, and sorrows of others. I need to be glad for their blessings and watch over them with love. After my friend leaves, I look up more Scriptures.

GRIEVING FOR THE GLORY OF GOD

Joseph hurried out and looked for a place to weep. He went into his private room and wept there.

(Genesis 43:30b)

I feel much better. I know others sometimes cry and mourn in private, and sometimes with others. I will not be ashamed of my tears in the future. When I'm overwhelmed with sadness, I'll let as many tears as necessary fall. I had better stock up on Kleenex.

I know that no matter how hard or difficult my situation/ circumstance is, and no matter how wild my emotions are, the solution is always found in God's Word. The Bible never changes. And God is watching with love and will dry all my tears.

He will swallow up death forever.
The Sovereign LORD will wipe away the tears from all faces.

(Isaiah 25:8a)

Biblical Friends

Biblical friends are godly people who love the Lord and seek to follow Him. They are filled with the Holy Spirit, who gives them the power to help them live a godly life.

They seek out people who are in need of comfort, support, strengthening, and encouragement. They lead the sad, lonely grieving person to applicable Scripture.

Your words have supported those who stumbled; you have strengthened faltering knees.

(Job 4:4)

If one falls down, his friend can help him up.
But pity the man who falls and has no one to help him up!"

(Ecclesiastes 4:10)

Instruct a wise man and he will be wiser still;
teach a righteous man and he will add to his learning."

(Proverbs 9:9)

Application

1. Do you let yourself cry openly, or do you hold back your tears when you are with others? Why? How do you feel after you've cried for a long time? Better? Worse? Discouraged? Peaceful?
2. What can you do when your emotions are out of control? To whom or what do you turn to?
3. Do you have a biblical friend who has or is currently helping you? Are you a biblical friend to someone? Are you willing to become a biblical friend to a grieving person today or when there is a need?

Return to God

January 2009

Superwoman is gone. I no longer live her lifestyle or carry her many burdens. She was a selfish, self-centered, annoying, irritating, joyless, unhappy, miserable person. Why did I let her hang around so long? Or even let her into my head in the first place? I had all the power and strength of Jesus; I don't know why I didn't use it to throw her out before she got such a strong grip on me.

I can do everything through him who gives me strength.
(Philippians 4:13)

Today, Lord, I admit I let myself be influenced by my feelings, emotions, and thoughts. And I responded in a way that was not pleasing to You. I was so very wrong. I let myself become separated from You. I want to come back, and I will never leave again. No matter what my trials or circumstances may be. You are my tower and my strength. You are my everything!

The name of the LORD is a strong tower; the righteous run to it and are safe.
(Proverbs 18:10)

I know, Father, I sinned against You when I turned away from You and looked only to myself. I was displeasing You. In my deep grief and uncontrollable selfishness, I let myself fall into a spiritual amnesia. I let the truths and promises of Your Word be blocked from my mind. Nothing I had learned or held close to my heart was able to escape from that darkened, empty space in my head.

Let us examine our ways and test them, and let us return to
the Lord.

(Lamentations 3:40)

Lord, I take full responsibility for my separation from You. And I am at
a loss as to what to say. I can only ask that You forgive me. I know I was
wrong, and I confess my sin and repent of it. I denounce my wayward
behavior that separated me from You.

I will heal their waywardness and love them freely.

(Hosea 14:4a)

I sincerely long to return to You, Lord. Your patience with me has been
endless. Don't give up on me now.

Let Your light shine again in my heart and mind. I need Your
Scriptures available for recall. Help me to remember those promises that
I relied on so often in the past. I will do my part to study, memorize,
and meditate daily. To pray faithfully. To praise Your Holy Name. All
glory is Yours.

Is any one of you in trouble? He should pray. Is anyone
happy? Let him sing songs of praise.

(James 5:13)

My greatest desire is to be surrounded by Your love in the safety of Your
sanctuary.

Application

1. When in your life did a situation, circumstance, or trial cause you
to separate yourself from God?
2. What sin do you need to confess today? When will you do it?

Ongoing Thoughts

$\mathcal{I}$ still want someone to listen to me and let me talk about Bud. I want to tell all about Bud—his illness and his dying, but also about Bud as a person. I know if I can tell my whole story to just one person, I can then forget it and move on with my life. But I just can't find that one person. Where are you?

Yesterday, while driving, I started talking to myself, as usual. Telling myself everything I've wanted to tell others. I just rambled on and on. I suddenly realized I was talking to my almighty Father. Telling God all the things about Bud that I've wanted to tell to others.

God always listens when I talk with Him. He is patient while I tell Him about the bad things, as well as the good.

This morning I want to find Scripture that speaks of God listening when I talk or pray to Him.

> Give ear to my words, O LORD,
>   consider my sighing.
> Listen to my cry for help, my King and my God,
>   for to you I pray.
> In the morning, O LORD, you hear my voice;
>   in the morning I lay my requests before you
>   and wait in expectation.
>
> (Psalm 5:1-3)

How uplifting it is to pray to God, to know I can pray anytime, anywhere, even as I drive. I have always prayed each morning. My mind seems freer from problems and distractions. I realized today that God wants my regular communication and fellowship with Him, regardless of time or place. I need to concentrate on Him throughout my day and into my evening. Thinking about fellowship/communicating with God took me to 1 John, verse 3.

And our fellowship is with the Father, and his Son, Jesus Christ.

(1 John 1:3b)

As Pastor has taught, I read the entire first chapter of First John. And I found another important verse.

If we confess our sins, he is faithful and just and will forgive us our sins and purify us from all unrighteousness.

(1 John 1:9)

Sin puts a barrier between God and me. My confession and repentance leads to God's forgiveness, and then the barrier is removed. It is often very difficult for me to reveal my sins to God. I would like to pretend He doesn't know. But I can't hide anything from God. He sees all, hears all, and knows all. God already knows each sin I commit. Because He is faithful to His promises, and because His love for me is unconditional, He will never push me away, no matter what I have done. His Word tells me that when I confess to Him, He will draw me even closer to Him.

I kneel and pray before I finish reading First John.

In Prison

I am the one who has been keeping myself in prison, keeping myself chained to the past. I let the sin of selfishness and self-centeredness dominate my thoughts, my feelings, and my emotions. It is true there were times when I walked in God's light, but then I slipped into darkness again. The darkness frightened me, and I prayed to get out. But I guess God knew I wasn't ready yet. He would show me a flicker of light when I read and studied His Word, which I do on a more regular basis now. But too often, I revert back to the past, turning to myself and wallowing in self-pity once more. When I do that, the light goes dim.

Please, Lord, do not keep me in darkness.

Of course, God isn't keeping me in darkness; I am. What I need to do is to seek God and hold fast to his truths.

> Brothers, I do not consider myself yet to have taken hold of it. But one thing I do: forgetting what is behind and straining toward what is ahead.
> (Philippians 3:13)

I need to forget the past, the things that continue to haunt me: my mistakes, my failures, and my unhappy memories. I don't want to be stuck in the past.

I can let go of the past because my hope is in Jesus Christ. I will no longer dwell on my past (or Bud's past). I want to concentrate on my relationship with God; I want to grow in his Word. I know God has forgiven me, and He chooses to forget my mistakes.

"For I will forgive their wickedness and will remember their sins no more."

(Jeremiah 31:34b)

Now with Your help, Holy Spirit, I can move on with my life in obedience to my Lord.

I am setting a goal to personally know Jesus Christ, my Lord and Savior. And I will not allow anything to take me away from my goal. On a daily basis, I will lay aside everything that is displeasing to God and harmful to me. This includes negative thoughts, feelings, emotions, and hurtful memories.

I will also leave behind anything that distracts me from living as Christ desires me to live—including my past!

Application

1. What is keeping you locked to the past? A person? Memories? An event? Thoughts? Why are you hanging on to these?

2. What do you need to confess to God about your past? How will this help you to move on with your life? When will you confess?

Dull and Sluggish

*I*n many ways, I have allowed myself to become dull and sluggish in my daily walk with Jesus. Why and how did I let this happen? I remember a Scripture from counseling with Katie. It seems I've had that problem before.

We do not want you to become lazy, but to imitate those who through faith and patience inherit what has been promised. (Hebrews 6:12)

It is the promises of Jesus Christ found in God's Word that keep me from becoming spiritually lazy and bored.

God's Promises

God, Your promises I hold so dear,
Remembering each, I keep You near.
Your love is unconditional and so very deep,
Your watch care continuous; You never sleep.
Your mercy is new every day,
And You hear me when I pray.
My prayers are answered in Your time,
And in Your mysterious ways, not mine.
Your grace is sufficient, all I need;
And by it I was saved, not by a deed.
Dear Lord, it is Your abounding grace
That saves me from the sin and evil I face.
I am weak, but You are strong;
Your Spirit is with me all day long.
You guide my footsteps one by one,

And make my path straight when the day is done.
Neither man nor situation need I fear,
With faith and trust I keep you near.
Now I know I'll never depart,
From the One who placed love within my heart.

Bad Lesson Learned

January 2009

I certainly have spent a lot of time learning a lesson that I never should have learned in the first place. And I learned the lesson very, very well. I spent countless hours learning how to make myself miserable.

I knew what was best for me. I knew the answers to all my problems. I could make all the decisions myself. Or so I believed.

Each day, I looked to myself. I would tell myself how terrible things were, pushing myself deeper into despair. I thought God could use some assistance from me.

I took my eyes off God, off His blessings, His protection, His provisions, and His promises. I thought I was more desirable than God. It was evident that I wanted to spend all my time with myself.

I know I must get myself out of the way completely and let God back into my life. I want His guidance, direction, protection, provisions, forgiveness, and blessings. I miss His presence in my life, and I miss His love. He has always been available for me. I'm returning to You, Lord; please take me back. You are the only One who is important to me. I am nothing without You. I want only to please You.

Your Word speaks to me:

No one can serve two masters. Either he will hate the one and love the other, or he will be devoted to one and despise the other. You cannot serve both God and Money.
(Matthew 6:24)

I know Jesus is talking about money. But this also applies to anything I put above, or in place of, God. I cannot love myself and love God also. As I meditate on this, I realize how foolish my thoughts, emotions, feelings, and behaviors have been.

A Few Days Later

It is taking me a little while to choose to completely put God ahead of me. Today I can say with sincerity and honesty that being with God is more important than being with me. And more than a thousand times better.

I now have quiet time each day with God before and after devotions, during prayer, and at study time.

Two Weeks Later

What a weight has been lifted from my shoulders. I just take everything to God, moment by moment. He takes it from me, guides me, and directs me in the right way to go. He is part of every decision I make. His Word tells me how much He loves me, and He will never leave me, reject me, or forsake me. I can depend on all the other promises of His Word which I have held on to for years.

Dear Heavenly Holy Father,

You are my Master. I am totally and unconditionally devoted to You. Only You are worthy of my praise. I praise and exalt You and Your Holy Name. I will live my life under Your guidance and direction; I will follow wherever You lead me, in obedience to Your Word. You are my one and all, my everything.

When you are in distress and all these things have happened to you, then in later days you will return to the LORD your God and obey him.

(Deuteronomy 4:30)

Application

1. Who or what are your thoughts fixed upon?
2. Whom do you spend the most time with? How is that time spent?
3. Are your efforts directed toward God as your Master, or toward yourself? Explain.
4. How often, and in what way, do you offer praise to your Master?

Spiritual Collapse

Grief Journal, September 2008

I am battered by Bud's death and this painful suffering. I am ready to physically and spiritually collapse.

Spiritual Journal, February 2009

I know now that my perceived spiritual collapse was the result of my own inner weakness and reluctance to seek God through His Word.

My soul is weary with sorrow; strengthen me according to your word.

(Psalm 119:28)

Lesson

I am weak, but God is strong. God's Word provides the guidelines and instructions I need; they will enable me to follow His rules and commandments. He will personally give me the strength to live by those rules and commandments. All I have to do is ask Him each day for the strength to go in His direction, to know and follow His will. God is at work in every part of my life, not just the grieving part. And the work He is doing in my life is for my good. Yes, grieving is painful, and I wanted the pain to stop. God is able to stop the pain, and He knows when it is time, when His purpose for the pain is fulfilled. In my weakness, I lost sight of God.

Today I have a new perspective and a new mind-set. I trust completely in God. My faith is strong, and even if the pain returns, I will not give into it. Because I know God is always with me.

When my prayers are confused and doubtful, the Holy Spirit will intercede for me, and my prayers will be understood and heard.

In the same way, the Spirit helps us in our weakness. We do not know what we ought to pray for, but the Spirit himself intercedes for us with groans that words cannot express.
(Romans 8:26)

In God's way and in His time, my prayers will be answered. It may not be in my way or within my time frame.

"For my thoughts are not your thoughts, neither are your ways my ways," declares the Lord.
(Isaiah 55:8)

Application

1. What painful situation are you praying about?
2. Are you confident that your prayers will be heard and answered? If there is not an immediate answer to your prayers, what will you do?
3. How do you see God's ability to turn your pain or circumstances around for your good? How have you seen this in the past?

Away with Superwoman

Grieving Journal Entry, September 2008

As I reread my entries from when I was in superwoman mode, I recognize that I did accomplish a lot of tasks and got many, many things done. But there was a terrible cost. I paid with isolation, depression, despair, and loneliness.

Spiritual Journal Entry, January 2009

God is so great. It is January 2009, and I am close to God once more. He only let me go on my own for a short time. He was watching and waiting, and when it was time, He took me back. All along, His Word was calling out to me. And that day last November, when I picked up my Bible and began to read and study, God called out to me, saying, "Welcome back, my child."

Not only did I seek God, but I fell in love with him once more, as Jesus said:

Jesus replied, "Love the LORD your God with all your heart and with all your soul and with all your mind." (Matthew 22:37)

I do my Lord, my God almighty.

I see now how He has always carried me, watched over me, provided for me, and protected me. He felt my hurt as much as I did. I realize that He experienced an even deeper hurt when I strayed from Him, seeking myself.

CONNIE SUMMERS

I have strayed like a lost sheep.
Seek your servant, for I have not forgotten
your commands.
(Psalm 119:176)

After I strayed, I repented.
(Jeremiah 31:19a)

Someday

February 2009

It is difficult, if not impossible, to be brave and to put on a happy face, when inside I'm trying desperately to hold back the uncontrollable tears that are hidden deep within me. I will not let them fall for others to see.

I am alone; even the radio cannot fill up the hollowness of silence that surrounds me. Silence like iron chains, holding me captive to my thoughts.

I think about today. It promises to be a long, lonely day, although yesterday was okay. I let my mind drift off to someday; a day in the future. I am waiting for someday to come.

Someday—when I won't hurt anymore.

Someday—when that broken relationship will be made whole again.

Someday—when I can stop pretending.

Someday—when all my "business" is taken care of.

Someday—when the confusion and sadness will be gone.

Someday—when I'm better, I'll cook, sew, read, and knit again.

Someday, Someday, Someday

I really need to stop this and focus on God's Word. I don't know what to read first. I find what I am looking for in Proverbs:

Do not boast about tomorrow, for you do not know what a day may bring forth.

(Proverbs 27:1)

As always, Solomon puts my mind to work. I can't think too much about the alluring thoughts of someday. Because if I do think too much and for too long, the thoughts of someday will draw me like a magnet into a never-ending waiting game. I realize someday may never come. But God has given me today. Today could be as good as any day will ever be. If I am to bring glory to God today, I need to live today to its fullest. Just step out of the confines of my mind and release my thoughts about the future. I cannot allow someday to destroy my joy in today.

God, I am asking you to lead me, and I will follow. Help me to concentrate on today.

I am tossing out all my thoughts of someday right now. Now is the time to put today into practice. But how? Each morning, as I begin my day, I must remember this day was given to me by God. I can waste it or I can use it for good. Whatever I do with this day is important because, when this day is over, it is gone forever.

Tomorrow morning, as I write about today in my journal, what will I see that I left behind? Will it be something good or something bad, something meaningful or insignificant?

I will strive to leave something that is pleasing to God. That way, when I read it the next day, it will encourage me to keep on keeping on. Each day, God grants us 1,440 minutes. These minutes are God's gift. All He asks is that I use them for His glory and that I don't waste even one of them.

God has not promised me tomorrow. Tomorrow—someday—is like a fog that has settled in but will be gone when the sun comes up.

Why, you do not even know what will happen tomorrow.
What is your life? You are a mist that appears for a little while and then vanishes.

(James 4:14)

When a crisis comes along or when something bad happens, I am very aware of the importance of each hour, each minute. However, as my ordinary routine flows smoothly along, I often forget that each day is another chance to live life. To start each day with enthusiasm for what the Lord has given me and what the Lord desires me to do.

Another thought about today: God's mercy is new every day.

It is of the LORD's mercies that we are not consumed, because his compassions fail not. They are new every morning: great is thy faithfulness.

(Lamentations 3:22-23 [KJV])

Today God has offered me another chance to live my life in obedience to Him. He wants me to choose thankfulness for His mercy and grace, and to be confident in His faithful care. I have hope because I know He will be with me forever and ever. This is my chance to make each day fruitful.

And we pray this in order that you may live a life worthy of the LORD and may please him in every way: bearing fruit in every good work, growing in the knowledge of God.

(Colossians 1:10)

Lost time can never be found again. I am giving each day to Jesus. I will let Him do with it whatever He desires.

Dear Lord,

I know not where today will take me, but I know You will be leading. As night falls, You will still be with me, protecting and providing.

Application

1. How did you use your 1,440 minutes yesterday?
2. How will the people you interacted with yesterday remember how you spent your minutes?
3. What loving thing did you say? To whom? What kindness did you show? To whom?
4. Are you glad or sad that yesterday is over? Explain.

Remember, God does not want any of us to waste time. Use your minutes to honor God.

Happiness Shared
As the day ends and nighttime falls,
I lay my head down and try to recall,
What did I do today?
And what did I say?
That brought happiness and joy,
To just one man, woman, girl, or boy.

Remember Things

February 2009

*H*ere it is February, and my mind is still clouded. I just can't remember things like I used to. I write everything down but still forget. What's wrong with me, God? I try hard to keep things straight, and I know I do remember a lot. But I just feel like I'm not "with it" at times.

Help me, Lord—take away the confusion.

Psalm 44:15 speaks for me:

My confusion is continually before me, and the shame of my face hath covered me.

(Psalm 44:15 [KJV])

I am not really stressed or anxious; I just can't remember things. I am praying, Father, that this is not a physical thing with my brain. I know You can, and will, help me.

For God is not the author of confusion, but of peace.

(1 Corinthians 14:33a [KJV])

God, You are a God of order and clarity. Help me to put order to my thoughts by throwing out all the junk that accumulates in my mind. I know it is because I put too many useless things in my mind. I am praying for clarity and understanding as I read Your Holy Scriptures. I will no longer become stressed or anxious when I forget something. I will simply rest in Your peace and ask You to bring to mind whatever I have forgotten.

> You will keep in perfect peace him whose mind is steadfast,
> because he trusts in you.
>
> (Isaiah 26:3)

Trusting God

February 2009

I've finished my homework from Katie: trusting God with everything.

I know I must put every part of my life, even the smallest detail, in the hand of God, my loving, heavenly Father. God knows exactly what lies ahead for me. And I can trust Him to be with me and to help me get through whatever circumstances come. My path today may be smooth and straight, or there may be detours and potholes; regardless, God will be with me, and together we will be victorious.

> Those who know your name will trust in you, for you, Lord,
> have never forsaken those who seek you.
> (Psalm 9:10)

God will never abandon me, if I continuously seek him.

God's promises do not mean that, just because I trust Him, I will be free from all suffering and trials.

What God's promises do mean is that God will never leave me. He will see me through whatever is happening in my life.

This is such a comforting thought, one I can claim and hang on to. I know, God, it has been hard to just trust in You and not try to control things myself. Sometimes it's like I'm on a teeter-totter: I'm up and trusting in You, and then I'm down and trying to take control again. Holy Spirit, please help me to remember God is the only One I can truly trust. I am putting my trust in my Holy Father.

March 2009

I have been studying more about trust. I know my trust in God is growing. I do trust in Him more each day. There is the occasional slip when I trust in my own ability and strength. That's when I fail. Katie has taught me well; I look for more Scriptures.

Trust in the LORD with all your heart and lean not on your own understanding.

(Proverbs 3:5)

Why is it, Lord, when I have to make a major decision, I look to myself instead of trusting You? Lord, You always know what is best for me. I know You have given me the ability to think and to reason. And I do. I plan ahead and think through my decisions. But the link I sometimes omit is You. I know You are much, much wiser than I. Starting right now, before making any decisions or choices, I will bring them to You in prayer. Your Word will be my guide. Your will be done, not mine.

God, I am asking You to lead and direct me as I make all my decisions. I will follow Your directions.

Then I will answer the one who taunts me, for I trust in the LORD.

(Psalm 119:42)

142

I Understand Now

All those days and nights of crying in the solitude of my home, by myself, without anyone, are over.

I was never alone; I just did not acknowledge the presence of the One who never leaves me.

I had let my thoughts, emotions, and feelings control me. I blamed my poor attitude on being tired and exhausted.

I let my vision be so blurred; I did not realize that God was right beside me, holding me up. He will never leave me, forsake me, or reject me. Because God has said,

"Never will I leave you, never will I forsake you."
(Psalm 73:23)

Yet I am always with you; you hold me by my right hand.
(Hebrews 13:5b)

What a picture. God is always holding on to me, and I am holding on to Him. I am continually in God's grip. He is my security. I feel secure.

Let the beloved of the LORD rest secure in him, for he shields him all day long, and the one the LORD loves rests between his shoulders.
(Deuteronomy 33:12b)

143

Still Struggling

February 2009

*D*ear Father, it seems as if I am doing really well. I am walking and talking with You daily, asking for guidance and direction. I am serving in church, caring for others, and attending Bible Study Fellowship. At times I enjoy my family and friends. I'm in Your Word every day.

But today I feel like I am still struggling. I think I have not been the person You desire me to be, yet I don't know how I've failed You. My thoughts are so mixed up. I know something is missing. I do try very hard every day to serve You. I study and study, and I know I am learning. Help me discover what I need and where I need to go.

And find out what pleases the Lord.

(Ephesians 5:10)

In my journal a year ago, when Bud was still here, I wrote: "I know dear heavenly Father, You have something wonderful planned for my life. And this time of caring and ministering to Bud is preparation for me. For You give me hours during the day to study and meditate on your word."

I still believe this is true today. But I still feel that no one really needs me. That people aren't interested in me or what I am doing. It could be because what I do is not very interesting, I know, God, You do not want to use me in this present state of mind.

Please lead me to the Scripture I need today.

Therefore, prepare your mind for action; be self-controlled; set your hope fully on the grace given to you when Jesus Christ is revealed.

(1 Peter 1:13)

Lesson

It is so clear what I need to do.

First, prepare my mind. This may be harder than it sounds. I think what it means is to clear all those useless, worthless, ineffective, counterproductive, fruitless thoughts out of my mind. To replace those thoughts with God's Word. And the only way to do this is by reading and studying, each day.

Second, I need to practice self-control. That is, to be disciplined in all areas of my life and to be obedient even when disobedience is easier.

Third, I must stay focused on Jesus Christ and prepare for His coming.

Put Off	Put On
Thoughts that contradict God's Word	Each day, meditate on God's Word before and after quiet time with God
Self-satisfying worldly behaviors	Read, study, and meditate on the book of Hebrews
Each day, be prepared for Jesus' return	Do what God wants me to do, not what I want to do. Show thankfulness for God's grace and mercy. Look up Scriptures on obedience.

Application

1. If Jesus came today, what would you say to him?

2. If Jesus came today, what would you want Him to say to you? What do you think He will say to you?

3. In what areas of your life are you being disobedient to God? What do you need to change? How will you do it? When will you do it?

Postscript, January 2011

In Sunday school, we just finished studying spiritual disciplines. In his book, *Spiritual Disciplines for the Christian Life*, Donald S. Whitney lists the spiritual disciplines:

1. Bible intake
2. Prayer
3. Worship
4. Evangelism
5. Serving
6. Stewardship
7. Fasting
8. Silence and solitude
9. Journaling
10. Learning
11. Perseverance in the disciplines

Negative Attitude, Be Gone

February 2009

I must get rid of the negative attitude that has dominated my life since Bud died. I know it is my decision to do so. I also know that negativism is displeasing to God. I would like to hide it from God, but I know I cannot.

Jesus has called me to be like Him. To be a servant like Jesus would bring great pleasure to my Father, God. This is what I desire to do and what I plan to do. I will not allow thoughts, laziness, or apathy to be part of my life any longer.

If I keep my thoughts positive, my actions/behavior will show my enthusiasm to others. I want others to see how excited I am about Jesus. And also that I am doing what he asks me to do. He is asking me to serve and give to others, both my time and my resources, in ways that will bring all the glory to Him.

You were ready to give; and your enthusiasm has stirred most of them to action.

(2 Corinthians 9:2b)

Whoever serves me must follow me; and where I am, my servant also will be. My Father will honor the one who serves me.

(John 12:26)

It is while I am serving, caring for others, and giving with pleasure and joy, that I reflect the character of Jesus Christ. All glory is for my Father, God.

Out of the Pigpen

I discovered, in my reading, that one failure doesn't mean my whole life is a failure.

My life is not a failure if I continue to repent of my sin and turn from it. God will still use me. Success often rises out of failure.

Because of the LORD's great love we are not consumed, for his compassions never fail.

(Lamentations 3:22)

Part of my failure arose from my isolating myself from others. I was trying to go it alone. God put many people in my life; I chose not to ask them for the help and comfort I needed.

Plans fail for lack of counsel, but with many advisors they succeed.

(Proverbs 15:22)

I will praise the LORD, who counsels me; even at night my heart instructs me.

(Psalm 16:7)

Asking for help from others is important; however, my first line of help must always be God. He is always available and knows my needs. He will provide and equip me. He also knows when and who I need help from; He will lead me to the person I need, when I need him or her.

I will always remember how I felt as I struggled while in that pigpen. I blamed everything, everyone, and even Satan for dragging me into that muddy hole. But I was the one who put me there.

When I took my eyes off Jesus and looked only to myself, I took that initial step into muddy darkness. With each selfish thought and with my self-centered behavior, I sank deeper and deeper. It was through neglecting the Word of God that I fell into the pigpen.

You have neglected the more important matters of the law—justice, mercy and faithfulness.
(Matthew 23:23b)

After much anguish, sorrow, and suffering, I finally called out to God for mercy.

Answer me quickly, O LORD; my spirit fails.
Do not hide your face from me or I will be like those who go down to the pit.
(Psalm 143:7)

With compassion, God pulled me out of that pigpen. His mercy cleansed me, and through His grace, I was forgiven. Now, with love and tender care, He is healing my broken heart and soul. Today there is joy in my heart, and I am at peace.

He lifted me out of the slimy pit, and out of the mud and mire; he set my feet on a rock and gave me a firm place to stand.
(Psalm 40:2)

God has placed me on a solid rock. He is making my path straight once again. He is guiding my footsteps. He promises that He will catch me if I stumble, and I will tightly grasp His mighty hand.

Though he stumbles, he will not fall, for the LORD upholds him with his hand.
(Psalm 37:24)

All praise, honor, and glory belong to my Lord and Savior, Jesus Christ.

Saying, "'Amen! Praise and glory and wisdom and thanks and honor and power and strength be to our God for ever and ever. Amen!'"

(Revelation 7:12)

Application

1. When have you taken your eyes off Jesus? What was the circumstance/ situation? What action did you take?
2. When and how did you return to Jesus?

The Wind

September 2009

Even I can see that sometimes my own efforts are just ridiculous. I try to do things my way and with my own strength. I am exhausted! It's like trying to rake leaves in a windstorm. For every few leaves I rake, a hundred more are scattered by the wind. I am struggling too hard, fighting that ever-changing direction of the wind.

Please God, give me the wisdom to stop trying to do the impossible. I can no longer rake against this wind; I need Your help. Let me hold on tightly to You until You stop the wind. I know You are in control of everything. I surrender my life to You and Your almighty power.

"So do not fear, for I am with you; do not be dismayed, for I am your God.
I will strengthen you and help you;
I will uphold you with my righteous right hand."
(Isaiah 41:10)

God gives me the assurance of His strength, help, and victory over my present situation, over the ever-changing circumstances of my life, and over sin and death.

He was delivered over to death for our sins and was raised to life for our justification.
(Romans 4:25)

Application

1. In what situation are you currently using your own strength? What are you accomplishing?
2. When in the past have you used God's strength to overcome a difficult situation? What did you accomplish?

Juggling Many Balls

I am juggling a hundred different balls, trying to keep them all in the air: serving, studying, Bible Study Fellowship, visiting, caring for others, celebrating birthdays, enjoying special occasions with family and friends, taking care of the house, doing yard work, etc.

Help me, God; all these balls are going to fall. I fear they will come down all at once and with tremendous force, right upon my head. *Plop! Plop! Plop!* The balls are gone! I am no longer juggling. I look down, and the balls are in a basket at my feet. I look up, for it must have been God's hand that put them there.

Father, I know that I can only hold one ball at a time right now. I will pick up one ball and hold it until that task or learning is completed. And then the glory will be Yours, as You show me, through Your power and strength, how I can keep all those balls in the air. Lead me, Father, to the ball I need to pick up first.

God is Great! He leads me to a ball marked "stillness". Before anything else, I must be still and let my mind rest. Spend quiet time with God. (Ball number 1: stillness.)

> Be still, and know I am God;
> I will be exalted among nations, I will be exalted in the earth.
> (Psalm 46:10)

> But the LORD is in his holy temple; let the world be silent before him.
> (Habakkuk 2:20)

As I silence my mind and meditate on these verses, I find that stillness brings peace. (Ball number 2: peace.)

And the peace of God, which transcends all understanding,
will guard your hearts and your minds in Jesus Christ.
(Philippians 4:7)

When I used to think about peace, I would think about world peace,
goodwill toward men, or having peace within myself or with others.
Some think peace with self is obtained by positive thinking or from not
having conflict or simply from feeling good.

God's Word taught me that God's peace is a very different kind of
peace. It comes from knowing and believing that God is in control of
everything. I know, without a doubt, that my future is secure. God has
promised me everlasting life in His eternal kingdom. There is no place
for anxiety to dwell within me.

The book of Philippians leads me to the book of John, where Jesus
talks to His disciples.

Peace I leave with you; my peace I give you. I do not give to
you as the world gives. Do not let yours hearts be troubled
and do not be afraid. (John 14:27)

The gift Jesus offers is the Holy Spirit, who gives me a deep and lasting
peace. It is a reassurance that God's peace will last throughout my life,
regardless of my circumstances or trials. When I have God's peace in
my heart, bad and evil forces (sin, doubt, anxiety, stress, and others)
cannot stay there.

This peace Jesus offers comes to me through the Holy Spirit. The
Holy Spirit is available to all who believe.

God can, and will, change me and my circumstances/situations; I
have only to put my trust in him. Through the indwelling of the Holy
Spirit, I can experience peace and faithfulness. (Ball number 3: Holy
Spirit.)

When the Counselor comes, whom I will send to you from
the Father, the Spirit of truth who goes out from the Father,
he will testify about me.
(John 15:26)

One last Scripture I want to meditate on today is Isaiah, chapter 32. I find that, so often, Isaiah talks not only of the present but also of the future. And so it is in these verses. Quietness and peace will prevail when God's kingdom is established forever and ever. (Ball number 4: hope for the future.)

> The fruit of righteousness will be peace; the effects of righteousness will be quietness and confidence forever.
>
> My people will live in peaceful dwelling places, in secure homes, in undisturbed places of rest.
>
> (Isaiah 32:17, 18)

Another day, I will pick up additional balls.

Application

1. When have you taken the time to be still before God? Completely at rest? How long did you remain still? How did you feel afterward? Relaxed? Peaceful? Anxious? Restless?

2. When will you take time to be still before God?

3. Are you juggling too many balls? Which ball do you need to pick up first?

Finding God Again

Everything about me just seems to be out of whack. I feel so desperate, and the pain is back once more. It is so deep; threatening to disable me for life. All I know to do is pray.

God, I thought all this was behind me. I've been doing so well with everything. Your blessings are abundant, and You have made my life so easy. I am trusting You with everything. What's wrong with me? Today, Lord, I'm asking for Your help. I need You.

> I call on the LORD in my distress, and he answers me.
> (Psalms 120:1)

Lord, I am asking You, what should I do?

> So what shall I do? I will pray with my spirit, but I will also pray with my mind; I will sing with my spirit, but I will also sing with my mind.
> (1 Corinthians 14:15)

> The widow who is really in need and left alone puts her hope in God and continues night and day to pray and ask God for help.
> (1 Timothy 5:5)

I have a wonderful way to communicate with God: my prayers. God speaks to me through the Bible, and I speak to Him through my prayers.

> Listen to my prayer, O God, do not ignore my plea; hear me and answer me,
> My thoughts trouble me and I am distraught.
> (Psalm 55:1-2)

And pray in the Spirit on all occasions with all kinds of prayers and requests.

(Ephesians 6:18a)

God delights in my prayers.

There are many parts to my prayers: demonstration of my trust and faith, worship, confessions, repentance, praise, adoration, thankfulness, and requests.

The LORD has heard my cry for mercy; the LORD accepts my prayer.

(Psalm 6:9)

He answered their prayers, because they trusted him.

(1 Chronicles 5:20b)

Praise be to God, who has not rejected my prayer or withheld his love from me!

(Psalm 66:20)

God hears every prayer and answers each in His way and in His time. He knows my name and every detail of my situation and my life. He is always available, and He will also send whomever and whatever I need. I know, too, that I can always find the advice and comfort I need to sustain me through this and future setbacks in God's Word.

Summer 2011

Now my prayers include praise, worship, thankfulness, confessions, and requests. I always pray for others before I say my personal prayers. While praying I often quote Scriptures or read psalms to God. I lift up this psalm to God every day:

Shout for joy to the LORD, all the earth.
Worship the LORD with gladness; come before him with joyful songs.
Know that the LORD is God.

It is he who made us, and we are his; we are his people, the
sheep of his pasture.
Enter his gates with thanksgiving and his courts with praise;
give thanks to him and praise his name.
For the LORD is good and his love endures forever; his
faithfulness continues through all generations.
(Psalm 100:1-5)

Application

1. When have you needed to ask for help? Who did you ask?
2. When you pray, do you only make requests? Asking God to do
   something for you or to give you something?
3. How do you praise God when you pray?
4. Do you thank God for your blessings each time you pray?
5. Do you trust God to answer your prayers?
6. If your prayers aren't answered immediately, what do you do?

Making Progress

March 2009

I study and study. I attend Bible Study Fellowship once a week. We are studying Moses. It's wonderful. This is giving me a chance to learn more from the Old Testament. And I am making progress. My mind is clearer, and I can concentrate (most of the time).

Father, I thank You for the many blessings You have given to me.

From the fullest of his grace we all received one blessing after another.

(John 1:16)

Resisting Satan

Since writing about being out of the pigpen, I've studied and searched more Scriptures. But reading and gaining knowledge is not enough. I must apply it directly to my situation and my life. I really never gave the Devil much study time. Oh, I know about him, and know I have been tempted; I've even given into temptation at times. One Sunday, Pastor talked about the Devil in his sermon, quoting First Peter.

Be self-controlled and alert. Your enemy the devil prowls around like a roaring lion looking for someone to devour.
(1 Peter 5:8)

He explained how lions lay in wait and watch for young, sick, or struggling animals which have strayed. Peter is warning me about Satan.

And do not give the devil a foothold
(Ephesians 4:27)

I must be mindful of Satan, for he is just waiting for a time when I am suffering, or feeling helpless, weak, discouraged, and focused on myself and my troubles. It is through my own weakness and venerability that he will snare me. He is lying in wait to pounce on me, using his deceitful lies to tear me apart, to drag me into his den of sin.

Put on your full armor of God so that you can take your stand against the devil's schemes.
(Ephesians 6:11)

I know I am being protected by God. The devil can't overtake me, as long as I stay close to God and obey His Word. I must be faithful and trust in Him.

And they will come to their senses and escape from the trap of the devil, who has taken them captive to do his will.

(2 Timothy 2:26)

The final victory belongs to the Lord; for that is when Satan will finally be defeated and thrown into hell.

There is no wisdom, no insight, no plan that can succeed against the LORD.

(Proverbs 21:30-31)

And the devil, who deceived them, was thrown into the lake of burning sulfur, where the beast and the false prophet had been thrown. They will be tormented day and night for ever and ever.

(Revelation 20:10)

Almighty God, all praise and glory will be Yours in victory.

We will shout for joy when you are victorious and will lift up our banners in the name of our God.

(Psalm 20:5)

Application

1. When have you been tempted by the Devil? What difficulty or problem were you experiencing?
2. How did you overcome the temptation?
3. Do you feel the Devil has control over your life? Who can help you? Who can save you?
4. Do you believe there is a heaven? Do you believe there is a hell?

Forgetting the Past

Last night, once again, I let the past over take the present. I know I need to forget the past. The things that burden me, those ridiculous and unreasonable notions I get in my head. I know they are just my overactive imagination. I take something that happened a long time ago, or a bad memory, and I turn it into a big deal. Like I'm the only one who ever made a mistake. I even blame myself for things that weren't my fault. And then I replay it over and over in my mind. It's just so crazy.

Now for today. Forget last night. I wrote awhile back that my goal was to know Christ. I even went so far as to write, "I will no longer dwell on my past (or Bud's)." So much for that.

I really do want to concentrate on my relationship with God and grow in my knowledge of Him and His Word. Why do I hang on to the past? I think it was just one of those bad nights. It isn't the end of the world. I can move ahead today, if I choose to.

I just need to spend some time with God, and with the help of the Holy Spirit, I can regain my balance and my sanity. I want to live my life in obedience to my Lord.

I ask myself the question Katie would ask, "What Scripture do you need right now?"

Give me understanding and I will keep your law and obey
it with all my heart.
(Psalm 119:34)

Your statutes are wonderful; therefore I will obey them.
(Psalm 119:129)

The unfolding of your words gives light; it gives
understanding to the simple.

(Psalm 119:130)

Your statutes are forever right; give me understanding that
I may live.

(Psalm 119:144)

Jesus replied "If anyone loves me, he will obey my
teaching."

(John 14:23a)

Now the hard work starts. To meditate on these and other Scriptures so
I can apply them to my daily life.

If I ask the Holy Spirit for discernment, He will give me
understanding, which will lead to knowledge and then to wisdom,
which will lead to obedience, and, finally, to application. Wow!

Almost Stuck Again

Last week I started to remodel the family room in the basement. I worked so hard ripping and tearing out that gigantic bookcase. It was a very difficult task. A tornado could have blown my house away, and that bookcase would still be standing. I had to use screwdrivers, pliers, a hammer, a sledgehammer, and a saw to demolish it. Getting the walls ready to paint was much easier, although very time consuming.

Today I wonder why I went to all that trouble. It won't change anything in my life. My attitude and thoughts are just crazy.

Just when I think I'm doing better, I let my thoughts slow me down. I go into slow motion, and I'm ready, once again, to just give up.

I am just tired; I try to rationalize (a worldly word). My mind is as numb as if it had been injected with Novocain. There is no ability to think or to feel.

I'll just sit here in the middle of this cement floor, among the broken boards, the dust, the ladder, the paintbrushes, and the buckets of paint. I'll just ignore the mess in my mind and the mess in my basement.

I know I can't give in to these thoughts and feelings, and I know I can't just give up. There is always hope. God is in control of everything, and I trust in my God.

I have a choice. I can choose to continue to sit here and cry, and to be miserable, or I can choose to look to God. Through God's strength and love, I can choose to go beyond these feelings and emotions. The ones that have been gnawing at me for so long. I have created my own troubles and struggles.

I am not the first person to lose a husband; nor will I be the last. This brings to mind my first memory verse:

No temptation has seized you except what is common to man. And God is faithful; he will not let you be tempted beyond what you can bear. But when you are tempted, he will also provide a way out so you can stand up under it.
(1 Corinthians 10:13)

I need to make peace with God. I kneel and pray. A heavy burden is lifted from me. I will not give in to this deep despair any longer, or ever again.

Come to me, all who are weary and burdened, and I will give you rest.
(Matthew 11:28)

Jesus is promising me love, healing, and peace with God. He is not promising an end to all my problems and troubles.

Father, I want to have a relationship with You, as I have had in the past. Help me to draw closer to You.

I know, Father, You were just waiting for me to say, "I need You, and I want You in my life forever." I know only You can change the weariness of my everyday problems into a spiritual purpose for my life. Thank You, Father God.

I pick myself up. I go to the phone to call Teresa. I ask her if she would like to help me paint. She says she would.

Thank You, God; You lifted that burden from me and blessed me with a daughter willing to help. And thank You for Your continuous, faithful watch care over me.

All the ways of the LORD are loving and faithful for those who keep the demands of his covenant.
(Psalm 25:10)

Satan Defeated Once Again

I remember when Satan had me in that deep well, pushing me under. Now I know it was with the first selfish thought, the first display of a negative attitude, that I needed to seek God. If I had sought God when the initial negative thought came into my mind, He would have rescued me.

After almost drowning, through prayer, I did ask God to come into my life once more. And He did.

Only God could pull me out of the well that Satan threw me into. God gave me the strength to climb up into his light and into his arms. It was You, God, who gave me strength to break down Satan's strongholds, which had kept me underwater. Your Word reminds me that You can, and will, destroy Satan.

The weapons we fight with are not weapons of the world. On the contrary, they have divine power to demolish strongholds.

(2 Corinthians 10:4)

I am out of that well. But even with the strength God gives and the help of the Holy Spirit, I must remain vigilant, ever watchful against another attack from Satan. I know he will attack me when I'm most vulnerable and weakest. I must not be deceived by his schemes.

In order that Satan may not outwit us. For we are not unaware of his schemes.

(2 Corinthians 2:11)

Satan's goal is to get me away from my living loving Father. He also rejoices when I do not spend time in God's Word. He is very aware that the gospel is his enemy. It is through God's Word that I learn the truth about Jesus Christ, my Savior, and also about Satan, my enemy and deceiver.

Underwater

March 2009

As I see where the weight of grief continues to hamper my fellowship with God. It keeps me underwater, with my eyes closed. I am unable to see the love of Jesus. Several anchors weigh me down: negative attitudes, selfishness, my sinful nature, and worldly cares and problems. They pull me to the bottom, where there is only darkness. I can't get loose: I am drowning.

Help me, Lord, help me! I feel the release of the anchors, as if the ropes have been cut. I float to the surface, where Jesus is waiting with open arms. He gently rocks me in the waves of his love. I feel secure; Jesus has wrapped His arms around me. He is holding me as a shepherd holds a lamb. I am secure in His everlasting arms.

> He tends his flock like a shepherd: He gathers the lambs in his arms and carries them close to his heart.
>
> (Isaiah 40:11a)

> The eternal God is your refuge, and underneath are the everlasting arms.
>
> (Deuteronomy 33:27a)

Jesus is my loving shepherd. He is gentle and caring. I can always rely on His power and his strength. He is my refuge, my only true security. He is always holding out His arms, beckoning me to come. He will catch me when all my unreliable, unsteady supports give way. Nothing—neither deep water nor difficulties/struggles—absolutely nothing can overcome me when I'm safely tucked within the everlasting arms of my Lord.

GRIEVING FOR THE GLORY OF GOD

Application

1. When have you needed Jesus to gather you in his arms? How did you feel?

2. Have you ever asked Him to hold you in His arms? Why or why not?

3. If you need Him today, what will you do?

Evaluation of Biblical Counseling

March 2009

I want to write a little more about the biblical counseling I received after Bud passed away, but I feel there is too much information to include. The knowledge, understanding, and application of Scripture have been of tremendous value. To describe the spiritual maturity I gained is impossible. I just do not have the words. I know I have much, much more growing and learning to do. But counseling gave me a firm foundation to build on—God's Word.

The best way for me to demonstrate the benefits of biblical counseling is to merely duplicate my final evaluation.

I started counseling in November 2008 and ended February 2009.

As I started to write this evaluation, I was at a loss, not knowing how much to include in a short summary (and have it make sense).

Written Evaluation

My goal, need, desire for counseling: how to grieve in a way that would glorify God.

As I was studying about hope, I learned several things. Three stand out:

1. Only one person can provide the comfort that restores your heart—the source of all true comfort—Jesus Christ.
2. As I see how weak and needy I am, I gain a deeper understanding of God's powerful grace.
3. The comfort God has given me is not only His loving ministry to me but also His call to me to minister to others. (This I have done in many different situations and with many different people.)

Assignments: My first assignment was to write what made the homegoing of Bud so difficult. (I shared this earlier in my journey, so I have not included it here.)

The next week we reviewed this. This led me to think about my thoughts and attitudes. I knew about putting off undesirable things and putting on desirable things. I learned this from Bible study with Ruth.

Now I was having to practice this and connect it with Scripture. The structure used was the following:

1. Identify the problem.
2. Identify what to put off.
3. Identify what to put on.
4. Find Scriptures for actions to take.
5. What I learned.

[AUTHOR'S NOTE: *In my actual evaluation, I did identify and elaborate on each that I had identified throughout about my counseling.*]

The "put off and put on" exercise is an ongoing process. I will add new ones as I identify them. And I will continue to evaluate the previous ones. Reviewing each week, adding new Scriptures/actions as needed.

This has been a wonderful learning experience for me. It caused me to look to God's Word for my answers, not to myself or others.

Memorization of Scriptures: In the past memorizing Scriptures was most difficult for me. But now it is easier, because I understand the meaning and importance of the Scriptures as they relate to me. I now have them available in my mind, whenever I need one for my own use or quote it for someone else.

Book: *Trusting God, Even When Life Hurts* by Paul Tripp. A great book. It is difficult to summarize all I learned from this book: knowledge gained and application to my life.

A very short incomplete list.

1. God is in control of everything, He is sovereign.
2. God is great.
3. God loves me.

4. God works out all circumstances of my life for my ultimate good.

These were not new to me. But now I have a clearer, deeper, understanding of what they mean. My trust in God has grown from reading this book and also from understanding His Word more than before.

There have been two recent incidences when I trusted God completely, placing my burdens (concerns) and cares upon him. I know that whatever happens, God is there with me and for me.

God is the only One I can trust totally. Now, each day in prayer, I give my life to Him.

I am looking forward to finishing this book. I have one chapter left: "God's Sovereignty and Our Responsibility".

Assignment: Schedule: To keep a daily schedule. Although reluctant to do so, I did it. And it was very helpful. It helped in keeping my life in balance and also in setting priorities.

Some general learning: So much of the "head" knowledge that I had learned was turned into applicable knowledge for daily living.

I read Scripture with a different goal. Not only to know what it says, but also to actually digest it, to learn how to apply it, to see what actions I need to take, how I can use this knowledge myself, and also how I can help others.

A really big learning—that I am never alone. God is always with me. (I knew this but didn't always remember.) God never sleeps; this is such a comfort to me. There is not a moment, day or night, that God isn't watching over me. I can always talk to God, and He always listens.

To glorify God is not just a passive statement. It is active action. In the past I felt that no one noticed what I do or say, so I didn't feel I was glorifying God. Now I realize, it doesn't matter if others see God's glory through me; God sees it. And if God wants others to see it, they will.

I speak more openly and freely about God: his attributes and what he has done in my life.

I now feel God has a bigger plan for me. And I've often asked Him to just let me know what He wants me to do. And I will do it.

172

After studying and talking things over in counseling sessions, I know right now what I'm doing what God wants me to do. He wants me to continue to do the little things and serve in little ways, get to know Him, learn His Word. That's His plan for me right now. I am satisfied with that plan. I will continue to do what I am doing, and continue to learn and seek new ways to serve.

Through this counseling, I have found peace. I know the truths and understand many more Scriptures. And most important, I know whatever I need, I can find it in God's Word.

(End of evaluation.)

God blessed me through this counseling. Giving me a firm foundation from which I can grow and mature. He has also given me another biblical friend, Katie.

Thank You, Father.

[AUTHOR'S NOTE: I strongly recommend counseling from a biblical counselor if you are having difficulties and struggles in your daily life while you are grieving. A biblical counselor can also help with any problems or trials, anything you are going through right now. He or she will take you to God's Word and point you to our great counselor, almighty God.]

But Jehoshaphat also said to the king of Israel, "First seek the counsel of the Lord."

(2 Chronicles 18:4)

To God belongs wisdom and power; counsel and understanding are his.

(Job 12:13)

Your statutes are my delight; they are my counselors.

(Psalm 119:24)

Out of Depression

April 2009

*T*hat soft summer breeze is once again swirling over me. However, today I am not depressed. And I am not willing to just sit here and do nothing.

Today I am thinking outside of myself. I'm wondering if God still wants to use me to help others. I know there are people around me who are hurting emotionally and spiritually, as well as physically.

God, I'm asking You to help me move with compassion and love to those who need help.

God is great! He leads me to reach out to others who need encouragement and support. And as I reach out to others, God reaches out to me and lifts me up.

I cannot remain depressed when I reach out to others to serve them.

God's soft summer breeze carries me out of depression and into the lives of many.

> We are hard pressed on every side, but not crushed; perplexed, but not in despair.
>
> (2 Corinthians 4:8)

Learning

Depression is one of the most common emotional struggles in the world today. In some instances, (*mine*), staying depressed was a choice. I could continue to feel sorry for myself, or I could fix my thoughts on God. I needed to make a conscious effort to meditate on God's goodness. When I did, God's love for me took my thoughts off myself.

GRIEVING FOR THE GLORY OF GOD

my troubles, and my grief. All I needed to do was simply refocus on God's ability and willingness to help.

God is the only antidepressant (*I need*). I am making the choice to study and meditate on God's Word.

To get away from misery, I will choose God's way. I will find people who need help, encouragement, support, and friendship. I will serve my God and others, wherever God leads me. And I will serve with a sincere, joyful heart.

It is the Lord Christ you are serving.

(Colossians 3:24b)

Application

1. What problems or worries are keeping you focused on yourself? What are your feelings right now?
2. Who can you reach out to today? Do you know anyone who needs help, comfort, encouragement? What personal action can you take? When will you do it?
3. Where in God's Word can you find help? Who can you share God's Word with today?

Trip Out West

Prayer Journal, June 5, 2009

Dear Heavenly Holy Father,

I thank you so much for the wonderful vacation. To see Your magnificent creation. The mountains, prairies, lakes, valleys, redwoods, Crater Lake, and so much, much more. It's just too much to describe and comprehend. It was a joyous time with lots of laughter. Trying to follow the map made for an interesting journey sometimes. And Bill's car getting hit was an event in itself. Luckily, no damage was done. I think we were in at least thirteen or fourteen different states. I sincerely thank You for that blessing. Also, for Bill and Katie inviting me to tag along. We had so much fun. I have so many wonderful memories and at least two thousand pictures. We were truly blessed to have Your watch care over us continuously. Thank You for keeping us safe and free of car trouble. I'm humbled by Your awesome creation. You are the divine Creator.

In Jesus' name I pray. Amen.

Journal Entry, June 6, 2009

Father, I am still recovering from being away from home for a three-week vacation. What a great time!

However, it was so very sad for me at times. When I would see all those magnificent sights, my thoughts would be, "Wait until I tell Bud." Then I would realize it was not possible to tell him anything. Coming home was difficult because Bud wasn't here. The house was empty and felt strange to me. I'm not sure I will feel comfortable traveling again. You know I have always loved to travel, but it's just different now.

Written Prayer

July 9, 2009

Attribute of God: God and His Word are absolutely true and trustworthy. (An attribute is an inherent characteristic of God.)

Blessings: There are so many; here are just a few.

1. I am becoming more and more controlled in my physical and emotional life.
2. A roller-coaster day, but God was with me every moment, leading, guiding, and protecting me; just knowing this is a blessing.
3. Spending time with Teresa and the boys, taking supper to them. (Teresa called to thank me, which made me feel great).
4. God helped me and gave me strength to deal with a very difficult situation.
5. Feeling grateful for Wanda, a true friend and godly woman, who opened her heart and home to me at 12:30 a.m.

Prayer, July 10, 2009

Dear Heavenly Holy Father,

I finally understand what You mean when You say to dwell on You and not on myself or my problems. Yesterday I worked on changing my thoughts about me to thoughts about You. I know this is what You desire of me. Help me, Father, to use the strength and power You have given me today, and also help me to stay focused on You and only You. Holy Spirit, help me to discern when I need to think upon a problem or do some planning, rather than just letting a troublesome circumstance roll over and over in my mind, causing me stress and anxiety. The situation last night was so very frightening and difficult. I thank You for Your protection and guidance. This morning I am at peace once again as I give You that burden, for I cannot carry it. It is too heavy and damaging to me. Thank You for your loving watch care over me.

In Jesus' name I pray. Amen.

Loneliness Revisited

June 2009

I reread my journal from September and November 2008. I wrote about how lonely I was. My loneliness was so great that it consumed my life. But today my mind is clearer, and I am able to concentrate. I have come to realize that I do have someone to share my life with: God. And He encourages me to share everything with Him, moment by moment.

What a joy it is! To know I can talk with God, anytime and anyplace, and He always hears me. There is nothing that I can't share with my God. And He listens. When I need answers, they are waiting for me in His Word.

I am spending more time in God's Word, and the counseling with Katie has helped me so much.

Although I still get lonely at times, I am never alone. God is always with me.

Turn to me and be gracious to me, for I am lonely and afflicted.

(Psalm 25:16)

My soul finds rest in God alone; my salvation comes from him.

(Psalm 62:1)

When I need God, all I have to do is call out to Him.

Then you will call, and the LORD will answer; you will call for help, and he will say: Here am I.

(Isaiah 58:9)

Prayer

July 24, 2009

Dear Heavenly Holy Father,

Thank you for old friends and the fun and joy of being with them yesterday. Today my prayer is for me. Please, God, help me continue to see You, and Your work in me, as the next month goes by. My thoughts and emotions sometimes do go crazy. I try to pretend everything is okay. I don't want to call attention to myself or have a pity party and be self-centered.

But You know me and my thoughts. I'm tired of pretending. You know I'm really missing Bud. I have the "knowledge of death" in my head. But my heart still hurts. Please, God, just stay close to me and help me heal.

In Jesus' precious name I pray, Amen.

Visiting Grave Again

August 2009

I am standing at Bud's grave. A year has passed, and today, for the first time, I am able to shed the overwhelming sadness that once weighed me down. My heart beats with joy as I silently thank God for Bud's salvation. A few tears fall, but I'm a peace. Praise God.

> Brothers, we do not want you to be ignorant about those who fall asleep, or to grieve like the rest of men, who have no hope.
>
> (1 Thessalonians 4:13)

I know Bud, in his heavenly home, is also at peace.

> Now faith is being sure of what we hope for and certain of what we do not see.
>
> (Hebrews 11:1)

This true faith helps me to see beyond the grave. God promises eternal life to those who believe in Him.

God's promises are true.

Father, I remember that day when I visited Bud's grave for the first time. I felt so helpless and alone. I did not look to You. Today I am asking for forgiveness, and I have repented.

> Have mercy on me, O God, according to your unfailing love;
> according to your great compassion blot out my
> transgressions.
> Wash away all my iniquity and cleanse me from my sin.
>
> (Psalm 51:1-2)

Also today, Father, I can sing my praise to You. You know my heart is filled with love for You. And I praise You for all You are and all You have done. I can see and feel how Your life-changing power has transformed me.

The psalmist has more eloquent words then I do. It is with sincerity and love that I quote him:

Shout with joy to God, all the earth!
Sing the glory of his name; make his praise glorious!
Say to God, "How awesome are your deeds!
So great is your power that your enemies cringe before you.
All the earth bows down to you, they sing praise to you, they
sing praise to your name." Selah
(Psalm 66:1-4)

Father, here are my own humble words of praise:

Praising God

Lord, to You I humbly speak,
Although my voice is soft and weak.
You know my heart is sincere,
And when I praise You, You hear.
Your Holiness, I cannot comprehend,
How a broken heart you mend.
The glorious sunrise, at the beginning of each day,
Tells me You are the Divine Creator in every way.
The Alpha and the Omega,
Always there when I need ya.
You are ever present, wherever I go,
This I know, for Your Word tells me so.

[AUTHOR'S NOTE: *I was attending a ladies' retreat in June 2010 in North Carolina. We were given ten minutes to express our love for God by praising him. Ladies danced, drew pictures, sang, wrote, or prayed. I chose to write this poem.*]

Vacation

August 2009

Home from Ginny's. Thank You, Father, for the safe trip to and from North Carolina with Katie and Shirley.

I really did have a joyous time with Ginny. What a blessing to spend a night with Susie in Greensboro. Thank You for the joyous reunion of two childhood friends. We talked and giggled like little girls all night.

Today I realize that I really did not keep my eyes focused on You, dear Lord. When I needed You the most, I let myself look elsewhere. Well, not really; I didn't look, period.

I did separate myself from communicating with You. Why do I do that when I'm away from home?

I have talked with You this morning, and I know I am forgiven. You always welcome me back. I know I did not seek You while on vacation.

Also, God, I need Your forgiveness for my negative attitude, which led to a very stressful vacation at times. I did not respond to the situations in a God-honoring, God-glorifying way; I let others influence my mood and emotions. This was an opportunity to be Christlike, to show my love and devotion to You. To be an example to others, reflecting Your character, and thus bringing glory to You. Instead, I choose to be self-centered, only thinking about myself. I did not put others first.

A lesson learned:

Be perfect, therefore, as your heavenly Father is perfect. (Matthew 5:48)

I know I can't be perfect. But I do aspire to be like Christ. I know I will continue to sin. However, I can separate myself from the worldly values that surround me. I need to strive to make God's desires my desires. I know, God, You want me to show mercy and love to others, just as Jesus did.

I am going to make it my goal to be more like Jesus. I want to gain spiritual maturity and wholeness. I know I will never be perfect until I reach heaven.

Dear friends, now we are children of God, and what we will be has not yet been made known. But we know that when he appears, we will be like him, for we shall see him as he is. Everyone who has this hope in him purifies himself, just as he is pure. (1 John 3:2, 3)

God, Your love for me is so great and unconditional. You even call me Your child. As Your child, God, I want to live as Jesus did, to become more like him each day. I will sincerely work at keeping myself, my values, and my behaviors in line with Yours and not with the world's. Help me to give up the world's way of thinking and acting.

Application

1. When with people, how do you present yourself? Do you try to fit in? How do you dress? Do you drink? Use bad language? Discard God's Word? Show concern and love for others?

2. How do you see yourself growing more and more like Jesus each day?

Worldly Thinking
O God, what I do,
Doesn't bring glory to you.
How can I accomplish my purpose in life,
When I dwell on my troubles and strife?
I cling to Your promises so true,

But when in the world, I don't follow through.
I read and study Your Word every day,
But with people, I forget what You say.
The answers I seek are close at hand.
Just open Your Word, each day have a plan.

No Fear of Rapids

September 2009

$\mathcal{B}$ud has been gone a little over a year now. Today I am determined, with the help of the Holy Spirit, to keep my mind on God and His creation. I will not be sad. Thinking of God and His creation brings back a happy memory: when Bud and I went to Niagara Falls (the American side).

The roar of the waterfall was truly majestic and breathtaking. To look at all the power of that river as it flowed toward the top of the falls and then crashed to the bottom with such tremendous force.

This memory also brought back a journal entry written a few months ago. I had described myself as being hurled toward the falls. Unable to stop the force of the river, I just let the mighty rapids take me over the falls.

A truth I've learned: God is greater and mightier than both Niagara Falls and all my troubles.

Now to him who is able to do immeasurably more than all we ask or imagine, according to his power that is at work within us.

(Ephesians 3:20)

It doesn't matter if a great waterfall comes into my life, real or imagined. No matter how large or powerful the rapids are, God is greater and more powerful. And God is also greater than my grief.

I lay aside my grief as I turn to my Lord.

Now in my mind I can visualize the falls cascading down, coming ever closer to me, but I am not crushed by their force. Instead, as the powerful, mighty water plunges to the bottom, the spray billows up and sprinkles a thin mist of God's blessings over me.

End of Journal Entry

Are you in a grieving situation and feeling as if you are being carried downstream toward the rapids?

Look up to the Lord.

God is the Sovereign Lord over all His creation. The entire natural world, the universe, and all creation obey His authoritative voice.

Without warning, a furious storm came up on the lake, so that the waves swept over the boat. But Jesus was sleeping.

The disciples went and woke him, saying, "Lord, save us! We're going to drown!"

He replied, "You of little faith, why are you so afraid?" Then he got up and rebuked the winds and the waves, and it was completely calm.

(Matthew 8:24-26)

Application

1. What difficult situation are you in today? What type of help do you need? Who are you seeking help from?

Suffering Alone

Each day, I learn how insufficient I am in trying to control my life. I tell myself I am able to battle these overwhelming circumstances that constantly come upon me, often not realizing that I bring some of them on myself. I try to carry all my burdens by myself.

No more of that nonsense! I can no longer manage life with my own strength. Although, God, You know I have tried and tried. God, it is from You that I can find the sufficiency to overcome my inadequacies and live my life for You. I desire a closer relationship with You.

Not that we are sufficient of ourselves to think anything as of ourselves; but our sufficiency is of God.
(2 Corinthians 3:5 [KJV])

Lessons Learned

God knew I would have to experience my total weakness before I could experience His strength and sufficiency.

As a result of my suffering, God taught me the lessons I could learn no other way.

God has a perfect plan for my life. However, God will not continue to lead me to accomplish His plan if I continue to put up barriers and construct detours, all of which take me away from Him.

God will help me break down the barriers and ignore the detours when I humbly and sincerely reach out to Him, confessing and repenting of my sins, asking for His forgiveness, and totally giving Him my life.

I bow to His Sovereignty.

Today I am putting myself aside and putting God in His rightful place: as my Lord and Savior.

An Enormous Project

December 2009

What was I thinking? Yesterday I read additional journals and some notes from the last year and a half. My mind is on overload; I'm thinking about writing a book. Am I totally crazy?

Is this a mountain too high for me to climb? How will I ever organize all this information—my thoughts, the learnings, the truths and promises of God's Word?

I need to just take a deep breath and stop questioning myself. If this is God's will for me, He will equip me with everything I need. The Holy Spirit will be with me, giving me power, strength, endurance, and the ability and find the words to write.

I must never leave God out of anything I am attempting to do.

I bow my head and pray:

Dear Lord, I don't know if this book will ever be completed, but You do know. I leave it in Your hands. I thank you for whatever ability/talent I have. It comes from You. I can do nothing apart from You. You are my all-powerful, almighty God. What I write is for Your glory; I seek no recognition for myself. I have written this book so everyone will see Your glory.

[E]quip you with everything good for doing his will, and may he work in us what is pleasing to him, through him Jesus Christ, to whom be glory for ever and ever. Amen.
(Hebrews 13:21)

Predicted Snowstorm

The first predicted snowstorm did not materialize in our area. There is only minimal accumulation, a thin blanket of white covering the ground.

As I look out my kitchen window, I see a broad streak of light traveling across the sky, surrounded by dark clouds. This reminds me that when dark clouds surround me, Jesus' light is always shining on me.

I sit mesmerized by the changing scene before me. Now the clouds are completely covering the light, but only from my eyes. For I know God's ever-present light is always with me.

I turn to see the view from my large living room window. God's creation from this view is different and unique. I see the trees' bare black branches. Each twig is distinct and easy to see, unlike in the summer when leaves cover the branches. The wind is strong, and the limbs and twigs sway back and forth, displaying God's power. Not one breaks, displaying God's care for His creation.

I am also God's creation. His Word tells me He cares for me more than He cares for the sparrows. What comfort I find in the world of nature God created.

Don't be afraid; you are worth more than many sparrows.
(Luke 12:7b)

God also provides for the sparrows and other birds by giving all his creation a home. He has given me the promise of an eternal home with Him in heaven. I know all God's creatures of nature will be with me also.

GRIEVING FOR THE GLORY OF GOD

Even the sparrow has found a home,
and the swallow a nest for herself,
where she may have her young—
a place near your altar,
O Lord Almighty, my King and my God.
(Psalm 84:3)

New and Different Day

$\mathcal{W}$hat a difference a day makes. Yesterday I studied 1 Peter, chapter 1, verse 13:

> Therefore prepare your mind for action; be self-controlled;
> set your hope fully on the grace given you when Jesus Christ
> is revealed.

(1 Peter 1:13)

Peter is saying to put my thoughts into action. To kind of tie up all the loose ends of my thinking. To reject what the world says and what the world does. And to stay focused on God and His mercy and grace.

During my morning routine (prayers, devotions, reading, mediating, journaling, etc.), I frequently forget that each day is a new day. Although I wrote in my journal about "someday," I'm often still thinking about yesterday—the past, not the future. I need to remember each day is another chance in life. And every hour is precious to God.

> Because of the LORD's great love we are not consumed, for
> his compassions never fail.
> They are new every morning; great is your faithfulness.
> I say to myself, "The LORD is my portion; therefore I will
> wait for him."

(Lamentations 3:22-24)

God is always faithful and will do exactly what He says He will do. Today God has offered me another chance in life. God wants me to choose thankfulness for his mercy and grace. I'm to be confident in His faithful care. I have hope because I know He is with me forever. I will pray for His direction and wait for His guidance.

[L]et the wise listen and add to their learning, and let the
discerning get guidance—
(Proverbs 1:5)

Postscript

In the summer of 2011, I found this in my journal: "After praying, wait
patiently with quiet expediency."

Application

1. When have you run ahead of God and found yourself in a very
    difficult situation?

2. When you ask for direction from God, do you wait patiently for
    an answer, or do you follow your own direction? Give examples of
    each. Be specific.

Enjoy Life

December 2009

I don't understand myself. I haven't learned how to enjoy life. Help me, Lord. I am very content when I'm at home or at church. But when I'm at special occasions, birthday celebrations, dining out, or doing anything with others, I am not relaxed or peaceful. I'm always thinking about being at home. Yet, when outings are planned, I'm excited and look forward to going.

I know, God, this isn't Your desire for me. You have provided so much joy for me, so many fun times for me to participate in. Why can't I just relax and enjoy all You have laid out in front of me? I need Scriptures that will help me. Today I will—No, right now! I will find the Scriptures I need.

So I commend the enjoyment of life, because nothing is better for man under the sun than to eat and drink and be glad. Then joy will accompany him in his work all the days of the life God has given him under the sun.

(Ecclesiastes 8:15)

[B]ut to put their hope in God, who richly provides us with everything for our enjoyment.

(1 Timothy 6:17b)

These Scriptures point out God's desire for me to enjoy all that He has blessed me with. To set aside the thoughts that keep me bound to my house. I need to cut the ropes that keep me tethered here. When I am with others, I need to be there totally, with all my mind and heart. I need to be involved in whatever is taking place. Enjoy the food and the conversations and any activities that are offered.

The Scriptures also tell me to enjoy the work God has led me to do. There is also a great warning about money. Not to put hope in money and not to expect money to give me joy.

I will seek to do more things with others, and I will keep myself focused on what is going on around me. I will not think about being at home; I will just let God lead me where I need to be and with whom. Only God can provide the kind of enjoyment I need.

Despondency Evaporates

February 2010

𝒜 watch as my despondency becomes nothing more than a vapor that floats up into the air and evaporates. I am amazed; I feel so wonderful. How did that happen? Well, I changed!

A few years ago in Sunday school, I learned all about attitudes. Somehow, over time, I forgot to remember what I had learned.

I learned that my attitude will affect every part of me—my thoughts, my behaviors, my actions, my emotions, and my feelings.

I may not be able to choose what has happened to me, or what will happen to me, but I can choose my response to every situation. And if I chose a God-pleasing attitude, I will be able to endure until my situation improves and is resolved.

> The Lord is close to the brokenhearted and saves those who are crushed in spirit.
>
> (Psalm 34:18)

The prescription for having a joyful life is to put into my mind thoughts that are loving, kind, and pure; thoughts that honor God. I need to dwell on the good things in my life.

> A happy heart makes the face cheerful, but heartache crushes the spirit.
>
> (Proverbs 15:13)

The proverbs of Solomon make me laugh. His wisdom is so down-to-earth, yet accurate. And I need to follow his advice.

In my old state of despondency, every day brought heartache and despair. But now I really do have a "happy" heart. I am joyful. My

GRIEVING FOR THE GLORY OF GOD

days are good. Each morning, I look for new ways to make my life worth living. I know trials and struggles may still come my way. But I have God's guarantee that He will be with me, giving me strength and endurance. And in His time, He will lift me up and out of my difficulties. He is sovereign and it will be His time, not mine. My hope and trust are in my almighty God.

God is my ever-present companion, and with the help of the Holy Spirit, I am able to keep my thoughts, feelings, emotions, etc., under control. When troubling thoughts come to mind, I will take them immediately to my beloved Lord.

We demolish arguments and every pretension that sets itself up against the knowledge of God, and we take captive every thought to make it obedient to Christ.

(2 Corinthians 10:5)

Application

1. What thoughts of God do you have that are God honoring?
2. What kinds of thoughts do you most often allow into your mind?
3. What thoughts do you dwell on when you are alone?
4. What changes in your thinking do you need to make? When will you make them?

Medical/Spiritual Comparison

February 2010

$\mathcal{Y}$esterday I had my annual physical. My doctor told me all reports and tests were excellent. What a blessing.

Say to him, "Long life to you! Good health to you and your household! And good health to all that is yours."

(1Samuel 25:6)

This morning as I'm praising God and giving thanks, I think to myself, *I really need a spiritual checkup, as well as a physical one.* God, I'm asking You to give me a spiritual heart scan. I want to make sure my attitudes and thoughts are the same as Yours.

Search me, O God, and know my heart; test me and know my anxious thoughts.
See if there is any offensive way in me, and lead me in the way everlasting.

(Psalm 139:23-24)

Although I have never had a CAT scan, a CAT scan found Bud's lung cancer. I remember how sad and fearful we were when we heard that diagnosis.

God, You are even sadder when I sin, because sin is more deadly than cancer.

Now God, I am asking for a spiritual CAT scan to detect any hidden sin within my heart.

Test me, O LORD, and try me, examine my heart and my mind.

(Psalm 26:2)

Each morning, I take vitamins and a low-dose aspirin, hoping to avoid illness and cardiovascular disease.

Yet, when I read God's truth, I do not always swallow those truths; I do not always let them be ingested into my mind/heart, so that they become a part of me.

Today I am going to feast upon God's Word until I am completely filled.

I have hidden your word in my heart that I might not sin against you.

(Psalm 119:11)

I will continue to get my annual physical checkup, in order to avoid a medical emergency or crisis.

However, it is much more important to be prepared with God's Word for spiritual emergencies and crises.

My son, pay attention to what I say;
listen closely to my words.
Do not let them out of your sight,
keep them within your heart;
for they are life to those who find them
and health to a man's whole body.
Above all else, guard your heart, for it is the wellspring of life.

(Proverbs 4:20-23)

Medical Records—Junk Bag

April 2010

 hat a relief! I am finally motivated to go through all those medical records and reports left from the years of Bud's illnesses. I am throwing away all of those medical records which I kept so methodically during his illness. Three boxes full of reports, test results, hospitalizations, lab reports, etc. In a separate box are all the daily assessments I did so diligently.

As I get out the first box I pray, "God, give me the courage to discard everything and the wisdom to know I don't have to keep any of it. And please don't let the reading of the material make me sad. I don't want to cry today."

God is so great! I felt no sadness. The Holy Spirit led me to throw everything away, without even reading it. Thank You, Father. This was a giant step forward for me.

Now I can walk into that room and be free of those sad memories. I will never forget those years. But now, God, You are helping me put those years behind me and out of my everyday thoughts. You knew when I was ready, and You watched over me as I discarded it all.

A time to keep and a time to throw away.

(Ecclesiastes 3:6b)

My junk bag is getting fuller. Praise God.

Walking a Tightrope

April 2010

Life is like walking a tightrope. Step by step, I walk across that thin, tiny, fragile wire of life. Before I even take the first step, God is directing me. He has taught me to discipline myself daily, to study the required readings, to learn the techniques that lead to obedience, to memorize the important details, and to recognize the need for balance throughout this walk.

He advices me not to carry harmful things: pride, my sinful nature, self-reliance, and all the other things that lead to disobedience. He wants me to take love, faithfulness, loyalty, trust, submission, humility, and all the good things He has given me. The burdens I worry about He will carry for me.

He has equipped me with His Word, His promises, His strength, and His power. He tells me there will be some valuable stops along the way. There will be time to serve, to teach, to witness, to pray, and to enjoy the many blessings which He will supply. Again, He assures me they are all part of His perfect plan for my life. He holds me with His right hand, guiding my footsteps which are firmly placed on the straight wire. He is my safety net, and He will rescue me if I should fall. He assures me that, although the wire is thin (narrow), it is the best and only way for me to go.

He will provide my daily bread and my living water. I will never be hungry or thirsty. There will be no darkness, for He will be my light. I will arrive on the other side at the time He chooses. For He is in control of everything.

My reward is everlasting life in His eternal kingdom, where I will at last hear the words, "Well done, my good and faithful servant."

Memories

Memories are priceless reminders of shared experiences. In times of sorrow they are wonderful gifts to cling to. I have no desire to forget my cherished memories; they are a joy and bring me much peace.

All my favorite wonderful memories are sealed in my heart. They are just waiting until I call them form the deep recesses of my heart into a magnificent image that plays on the big screen in my mind.

I can, and do, remember the joyous times of my life with Bud. Our first official date (a hayride), our first kiss, the birth of our children, being reunited with all of Bud's children (Mike, Glenda, and Debbie), building our house, vacations (just our family and also with others), family meals together, quiet walks in the woods (holding hands), working hard together, hugs and kisses, sitting on the deck sharing thoughts and feelings, making plans, and on and on.

There are so many more memories that flood my mind, bringing a sense of pleasure and contentment. These I will save to be remembered later.

Occasionally there is a sad memory; Bud's illness or a difficult situation or phase we went through. These are fleeing, taken away by God's loving hands.

There are times when I do let them linger for a short time, for they are reminders of God's grace and mercy.

God always brought us through each situation, difficulty, or hardship in life.

Quickly God provides a gust of wind that carries those sad and painful memories away; they float farther and farther away, until they are remembered no more. My loving Father has closed my mind to the hurts and sadness of the past.

Banquet or Picnic

May 2010

I am facing a debilitating test: grief without help. I put family relationships and friendships on the back burner. I wanted them to step up and do the cooking, and I would just sit back and eat. I couldn't cook because I might get burned. But no matter what they served, it wasn't satisfying.

I wanted a banquet, but they were offering a picnic. At the banquet I expected fun, gaiety, laughter, and tables laden with desserts. I imagined the picnic would have little food, no desserts, and very little water. There could even be an invasion of ants.

Oh my, I sure spent a lot of wasted time in that kitchen of grief. Of course, family and friends did cook for me, putting love and care into each dish. I was so afraid of being burned for "caring too much" that I just did not accept the food.

Desserts are a comfort food for me. I know now I didn't need a banquet. I needed the picnic which they prepared and served with love. The down-to-earth comfort of family and friends who genuinely care for me. I had it all!

God sets the lonely in families.

(Psalm 68:6a)

They each provided comfort, support, and help in their own individual way.

Now I am offering my family and friends a feast. I will prepare it with love. I will serve each of them with thankfulness. I am asking God to bless each and every one of them.

"Come anytime," I would tell them. "The door is open, and I'll leave the light on for you."

Little Gray Tractor

This morning I'm thinking about Bud and his gray tractor. He loved all his equipment.

As I think about that tractor, I laugh; I am a lot like that little gray Ford tractor.

We both have had several years of hard work, yet we are dependable. There have been times when we had trouble starting. Sometimes all our cylinders do not fire correctly, causing us to stall and just give up. There have been a few times when we've run out of gas before the work and/or day was done.

The little gray tractor's paint is peeling, and it has a few dents. I have wrinkles and a few scars. We both have plowed through some very tough dirt and become muddy. But we always remained faithful.

There are some differences also. Mr. Tractor is loud and noisy; I am quiet and soft-spoken. But when called upon to serve, to help, or to be on standby, you can depend on us. We're always ready!

My silliness is over. Now I must start my motor and answer God's call for the day.

Wrinkles

The face in the mirror, how can it be?
A million wrinkles, it can't be me!
I look real close, then turn away,
I'll face that mirror another day.
But day after day, I look and sigh,
Those wrinkles, they just multiply.
Some say wrinkles are a sign of wisdom,
But they are the ones who don't have 'em.

My Garden

June 2010

There are always new challenges in my garden. There may be no rain or too much rain. My favorite plant may die for no reason. The deer may eat my hosta. And the birds may eat all my strawberries, just as they ripen. And that vine I thought was so pretty became invasive and took over my rose garden. The weeds multiply faster than I can pull them out.

Just like my garden, my life also has many challenges. Everything in my life is ongoing, yet continually changing; especially my relationships with family, friends, and even God.

To me, relationships have always been important. I value my family and friends. Unfortunately, during my dormant time of grieving, there were times when I wanted to put my relationships in sleep mode, just as my flowers sleep in the winter.

Even though I did not reach out to them, they showered me with dozens of flowers, showing love and caring.

I would think about calling but then make excuses to myself; in the end, I wound up not calling.

I have stacks of cards bought for a "special" person that I have never addressed or mailed.

I continue to seek an easy way to keep my relationships intact and ongoing. I want them to grow and bloom, but I don't want to do the maintenance required.

But maintenance is what I must do.

Today I am planting new seeds in my heart and mind.

Do not be deceived: God cannot be mocked. A man reaps what he sows.

(Galatians 6:7)

I must choose which kind of seeds I will plant: Seeds to please my own desires, which will result in a harvest of sorrow and sadness. Or seeds to please God, which will result in peaceful joy for me, a strengthened bond with family/friends, and a harvest of unfailing love.

I will plant God's seeds so I can cultivate my relationship with each special person in my life.

Let us not become weary in doing good, for at the proper time we will reap a harvest if we do not give up.

(Galatians 6:9)

I'll do the hard work that is necessary to keep in touch on a regular basis, and I will offer each person I care about a specially picked bouquet of my best flowers: a flower of love, a flower of caring, a flower of friendship, a flower of joy, a flower of peace, a flower of patience, a flower of kindness, a flower of goodness, a flower of gentleness, and a flower of self-control.

The fruit of the Spirit is love, joy, peace, patience, kindness, goodness, faithfulness, gentleness, and self-control. Against such things there is no law.

(Galatians 5:22-23)

God help me to be a gardener like You when I'm caring for family, friends, and others. Show me how to guide them to Your Word, just as You guide me. Help me to meet their needs and still point them to You, who will satisfy all their needs. I want to help them become stronger emotionally, physically, and spiritually, as much as I am able. And then, God, give me the wisdom to turn the strengthening over to You. I will lead them to You, Your provisions of daily bread, and Your fountain of living water which never fails. I know You will welcome them and care for them as You do all Your beloved children.

Heavenly Father, I thank You for my family, my friends, and my garden.

You are the holy, faithful gardener.

The Lord will guide you always;
    he will satisfy your needs in a sun-scorched land
    and will strengthen your frame.
You will be like a well-watered garden,
    like a spring whose waters never fail.
(Isaiah 58:11)

Caring Family and Friends

Dear Lord, let me always be mindful of all the special people You have put in my life, all those who love me.

A much overdue acknowledgment and apology to all my family, friends, and church family who loved and cared for me. There was much support given by family and friends through Bud's illness and at visitation, the funeral, and luncheon. There are many who have continued to offer support. Each one was helping in his or her own way. I just didn't see it or appreciate it during those dark, dark days. I had built a glass dome around my heart. I thought if I acknowledged any feelings, the glass would shatter and pierce my heart, and the pain would come back, even more violent than before. I felt I had to protect myself.

God blessed me. These special people never gave up on me. They continued to help and be there for me. At that time, I just wanted more. I expected them to walk a tightrope. To be able to balance my needs with their lives, to never fail to pick me up if I should fall.

If one falls down, his friend can help him up.
But pity the man who falls and has no one to help him up!
(Ecclesiastes 4:10)

I am truly ashamed of my past thoughts of family and friends. I often complained to myself that no one cared or thought about me. I held so many pity parties for myself. I know my thoughts and feelings were wrong. Excuses won't change anything, so I won't offer any. I ask only for forgiveness from each family member, friend, and church member who did help.

I pray, Father, You will bless each one, as I now recall the love and care they blessed me with.

Before Bud Passed Away

Wanda's frequent visits and phone calls; leading me to Scriptures.

Teresa stayed to help care for her dad; she was with us for ten days.

My cousin, Katie, came almost every day and stayed some nights during the last week. She intervened with hospice for me. When Les and Kathy were visiting from Illinois in July, she brought supper for us.

The visit from Les and Kathy was special. Les and Bud shared so many memories of days gone by, a true blessing for Bud.

Church family brought supper to us for a week. Thanks to Wanda, Melodie, Theresa, Pat, Joyce, and Dawn.

Chuck (church friend) said to call anytime if I needed help; he even gave me his cell phone number.

Shirley came to stay with Bud so I could go to church. (I wasn't able to go, but she stayed and visited.)

Shirley and Kathi brought leftovers from a family picnic that I couldn't attend.

Joel brought me Pastor's sermon; the timing was perfect, and he helped me with a very, very difficult situation.

Sue visited to offer support, and she also went to Borgess to pick up meds for me.

Family came to spend Sunday afternoon with Bud and me; this turned out to be his last Sunday.

Butch and Nancy came a couple of nights before Bud passed away; they were here while I was giving meds to Bud. Butch watched over me, and Nancy kept time for me. (I had to administer the meds every five minutes.)

Funeral Week

Lots of hugs and kisses.

Butch and Nancy came; they helped put all the furniture back in place and also stored the equipment.

Teresa helped with making the arrangements and ordering the flowers.

Wanda and Tanner cleaned out the refrigerator and did other cleaning

Shirley and Kathi helped clean house.

Food brought by Anna (pizza) and Bea (squash casserole) helped sustain us. Katie also brought food (ham, bread, and my favorite cherry pie). Danny brought two ice cream cakes. Teri brought lasagna and extra chairs. Nancy brought spaghetti and brownies.

Mike, Jonalyn, and their kids came from Florida. They brought four dozen roses. It was wonderful seeing Sharon, Bryan, and Brandan (my grandchildren) again.

Family from Illinois came too. Les and Kathy brought Mary with them. The three of them stayed with me. Les asked about my financial needs in a caring and concerned way. Kathy's laughter, which is so contagious, always makes me laugh too. We've shared so much. Pete, Dottie, Jessica and David also came from Illinois. Pete came even though he was not feeling well. (Wanda graciously opened her house to them.)

A bag of Peanut M&M just showed up. It's a favorite of mine. So many attended the visitation and the funeral. An abundance of flowers and cards. One card that meant a lot to me came from Dr. Hunt (family doctor). Inside the card he wrote, "Your love for Bud was amazing."

Flowers came from so many people. I kept the shooting star plant from Anita and Scott as a houseplant. I planted two rose of Sharon bushes from Dawn and Teri. Bill and Katie sent an artificial arrangement that now sits on my coffee table. I took the cut flowers and put them on Grannie and Grandad's grave (Bud's parents). All the flowers were beautiful. There were many contributions to the Augusta Library and also to my church.

Pastor's message at Bud's funeral was beautiful.

Greg prepared and delivered the eulogy. Very personal, capturing Bud's childhood and later years.

Sue sang at the closing ceremony at Fort Custer National Cemetery.

A funeral luncheon was prepared by the ladies of my church.

Days, Weeks, and Months after Bud's Death

This is where it is difficult to remember everything everyone did. So many did so much.

Butch helped clean up the yard and move all the equipment. He did several repairs around my house. He also built things for me. The biggest job was cleaning out the garage and hauling away all the junk. He sold things for me and helped me shop for needed items. (Sorry, Butch, my memory has failed me, once again. I can't recall all that you did.) I just know Butch was always here when I needed him, only a phone call away.

Nancy joined in on some of the things Butch helped with, especially shopping. She helped most with teaching me how to use my computer. (And her job isn't over yet!) She sold my things at her garage sale. She also included me in family get-togethers and arranged special outings. Our vacations continued as before.

Katie and Bill kept in touch, calling frequently. They had me over for supper and family gatherings. Bill called when there was a tornado warning for Augusta (as did Scott). They also invited me to join them on vacation.

Shirley called many, many times. We had lunch together, did Bible study together, and she sent many cards. I was also invited to many family gatherings.

Ruthie, Lu, and Kay (nursing school classmates) were incredible. Instead of coming to the funeral, they came a couple of weeks later so that they could visit with me. I read the eulogy to them, and Kay treated me to lunch. They came again, and then we resumed to our regular luncheons. What a blessing to have the support of friends since 1958.

Terry Lee removed a lot of junk from down back. He cut up a couple of fallen trees and did other odd jobs. He also painted two bedrooms and helped remove old carpet.

Tanner often stays with me, and we work in the yard. He and I do a lot of things together. A favorite when he spends the night: we always watch *Jeopardy* and eat at Burger King.

Teresa and Belinda helped me paint the family room. Teresa and Terry Lee helped clean the basement.

Wanda and I remain close, as we share many experiences together. She has always been there for me. We travel together. People often think we are sisters.

Buddy, a friend of Bud's, has helped with many major remodeling projects. He's always willing to come if I have a problem, and he often calls to see if I need anything. Margaret, his wife, also calls.

Susan and Skip are special. Susan and I have become very close and enjoy the time we spend together. We share a love of gardening. Skip always buys my coffee and delivers rocks for me.

Laura, my great-niece, calls frequently from Kansas, relating fun things about her kids.

Les and Kathy, cousins from Illinois, also call frequently. I visit them often.

Ginny sent many cards and called many times from North Carolina. I try to visit her and Eddie once a year. She often sends little gifts too.

Ruthie and Glenn called often. We also got together for lunch, talking and sharing. They showed much love and concern.

Katie P., my biblical counselor, I cannot thank enough. Our sharing of both personal and spiritual things means so much to me. She is a true Biblical friend.

Darrell and Mary (neighbors) both have watched over me and my house, concerned for my safety. Darrell put up outside lighting. Mary sent over a spaghetti supper one night.

I hesitate to end this page, as I fear I have forgotten someone whom I will then offend. During that difficult time, I know there were many things I forgot. My mind did not cooperate, and I may not have written down a name or what a person did for me. Please forgive me and know that I would never deliberately fail to acknowledge anyone. Everyone has continued to be so kind, and I truly appreciate everything that was done for me.

All the personal love and care that has been lavished upon me I can never repay. So I end as I began, with this prayer: Dear Lord, let me always be thankful and mindful of all those special people You have put in my life, all those who love me.

I have not stopped giving thanks for you, remembering you in my prayers.

(Ephesians 1:16)

Memory Garden

May 2010

I've tried so hard to forget the pain and hurt that I let my memories of Bud fade into a state of forgetfulness.

Today I am choosing to remember.

To remember all the love and fun we shared. All the good times, but also how we weathered the bad times together. And this summer I will plant for-get-me-nots for him in my garden.

And I pray, Dear Lord, I will for-get-not Bud.

I have planted flowers, plants, and trees in remembrance of many loved ones over the years, and also to honor the living:

Hibiscus: I planted these for Bud. He loved to see them from the kitchen window. This year I will plant two more hibiscus, especially for Bud.

Daisies: I planted these for my dear friend Nancy. They were her favorite flower; she was a very special person and a wonderful friend. (This is a late friend, not my sister-in-law.)

Daisies: I planted these for Aunt Reva. I did not know her during my childhood, but she became my favorite aunt once we met. She was not a "flower person"; she only liked daisies. She did love gifts, though.

Moon Flowers: I planted these for Aunt Mary who was one of my favorite childhood aunts. The flowers I grow are from seeds from her garden, given to me by my cousin, Katie.

Dahlias: I planted these for Uncle Harold, one of my favorite uncles throughout my life. Dahlias were the only flower he liked. The weeds that grow in my garden bring back a special memory.

Bleeding Heart: I planted these for my wonderful Grandma. I loved her so much; she was so caring and wise. She grew the most beautiful bleeding hearts in her garden. I get my love of gardening from her and Grandpa.

Roses: I planted these for Grandpa. He died when I was twelve. But I remember his beautiful roses growing up a trellis attached to the back porch of his house. And his round cement fishpond filled with goldfish.

Gladiolus: I planted these for my Mom who loved "glads," as she called them. She grew several rows every year.

Tomatoes: I planted these for my dad. He grew bushels of tomatoes and vegetables, but no flowers.

Weeping Cherry Tree: I planted this for Mary, my best friend. My family gave me the tree in remembrance of her. We shared so many wonderful experiences.

Rosebush: I planted this for Aunt Fonda, a beloved aunt. I brought it from her home in Illinois. She was devoted to her Lord and Savior.

Rose of Sharon: I planted this for Sharon, my granddaughter, after her near-drowning accident. She is doing well now.

Irises: I planted these for Fran, Bud's cousin's wife; she painted me a picture of a bouquet of irises.

Lilies: I planted these for my "fun" aunt, Aunt Lillian. She was the comedian of the family.

Lavender: I planted this for Donna, Bud's cousin's daughter. She loved country music and her kids.

Hens and Chickens: I planted these for Uncle Red, Bud's uncle. He and I used to play cards, and he would always try to cheat—a family joke. I don't know if he even liked flowers, but I planted hens and chickens because he lived in the country in Illinois.

Creeping Charlie: I planted this for my cousin's husband. No special reason, just the name. He would be pleased.

Lilacs: I planted these for Lorraine, the mother of my niece Lorraine and I became friends in our later years.

214

Baby's Breath: I planted these for Laura and Dustin, an unborn baby now in heaven.

Father, You are the great gardener. Just as my plants need me to feed and water them, I need Your daily bread and Your living water to sustain me.

Empty House

My house has felt so different without Bud. Empty, vacated, unoccupied—as if it was left unattended and abandoned. As I would wander from room to room, I wouldn't see what was there; I would only see what wasn't there: Bud.

I would often sit on the deck and remember when we built the house. I designed it. Although we had a contractor build it, Bud supervised the work. He made sure it was built sturdy and strong and on a firm foundation. While sitting and remembering, I would go through the album of old photos I had taken while building the house. Pictures from the first shovel of dirt to the last nail that was pounded in. My favorite one is of Bud standing between the upright two by eights that would eventually become the supports for the walls.

A multitude of memories would come rushing through my mind: Bud, house, kids, Bud, parents, Bud, vacations. I knew I had to stop these flooding images.

I knelt and prayed:

Lord, help me accept these changes that have happened in my life. Give me a spirit of hospitality that beckons family and friends to come in and sit a spell. Help me fill my house with love, so all who enter will be blessed. Fill my heart with joy and anticipation of new memories, as well as remembrance of sweet memories of the past.

It was then that I realized, it is not the house that makes a home, it is the family—my kids, grandkids, family members, friends, visitors, and me. Although Bud is not here, I still have many pleasant memories. I can keep him in my heart and mind.

It is now family and friends that will make my house a home. Together, we all will make many new and wonderful memories. I want

GRIEVING FOR THE GLORY OF GOD

my home to be filled with joy, peace, and happiness once more. So all who enter will know God lives here.

But as for me and my household, we will serve the LORD.
(Joshua 24:15b)

Stamp

July 2010

I'm stuck, much like a stamp stuck on an envelope. And just as a stamp can travel many, many miles, so can I. But I don't! All I need to do is begin; first just do it, and then stick to it. Pastor always says, "Just get over it and do it." I will stop all the excuses that only get me to the wrong place.

Therefore, my dear brothers, stand firm. Let nothing move you. Always give yourselves fully to the work of the LORD, because you know that your labor in the LORD is not in vain.

(1 Corinthians 15:58)

Father, You know I am very busy. I really don't waste time. But what I don't do is the routine, everyday, boring things. I do them, just not as often as needed.

And Lord, anything You ask of me I try to do, and I always try to do the best I can. I do it with sincerity and love. Holy Spirit, help me to do all the things that need to be done.

[A]nd to find satisfaction in his toilsome labor under the sun during the few days of life God has given him—for this is his lot.

(Ecclesiastes 5:18b)

God Picks Up the Pieces

August 2010

I wrote of when I exploded and felt like Humpty Dumpty. Today I can laugh at that image. And I see how ridiculous that was. Of course, all the kings' horses and all the kings' men could not put me back together again.

But my almighty King can—and does.

Today, Lord, I am admitting my failures and my broken spirit. I know You are the great almighty King, my Lord and Savior, who can repair and restore my broken spirit. No matter how many broken pieces there are, with mercy and faithfulness, piece by piece, You will make me whole once more.

My answers are found in Your Word:

If we are faithless, he will remain faithful, for he cannot disown himself.

(2 Timothy 2:13)

Today, Lord, please help me to find joy in all that You have put before me.

God, You who created me know me better than I know myself. And You never give up on me. I've made some wrong choices; I've let my thoughts and feelings control me. You know I have struggled and struggled with myself and within myself. Made mistakes and made my life difficult and troublesome. But You are faithful and merciful, and by Your grace You have chosen to forgive me and forget my mistakes. I have placed the truth of Your Word in my heart.

I will remember, God, You work in everything, not just isolated situations. And every situation is for my good. God, You are in control of everything. You can turn every situation around for my future good. You work within me to fulfill Your purpose for my life.

"For I know the plans I have for you", declares the LORD, "plans to prosper you and not harm you, plans to give you hope and a future."
(Jeremiah 29:11)

God knows the future. And as I see Him making me whole once again, it's like He is giving me a new beginning. As I live by God's Word and follow His leading, God promises me a wonderful future filled with hope.

There is surely a future hope for you, and your hope will not be cut off.
(Proverbs 23:18)

Hope is expecting something. It can be a thing hoped for or the act of hoping.

The faith and love that spring up from the hope that is stored up for you in heaven and that you have already heard about in the word of truth, the gospel.
(Colossians 1:5)

Praise be to the God and Father of our Lord Jesus Christ! In his great mercy he has given us new birth into a living hope through the resurrection of Jesus Christ from the dead.
(1 Peter 1:3)

My hope comes from God.

May the God of hope fill you with all joy and peace as you trust in him, so that you may overflow with hope by the power of the Holy Spirit.
(Romans 15:13)

My hope comes from God's grace.

May our Lord Jesus Christ himself and God our Father, who loved us and by his grace gave us eternal encouragement and good hope.

(2 Thessalonians 2: 16)

My hope comes from God's calling.

I pray also that the eyes of your heart may be enlightened in order that you may know the hope to which he has called you, the riches of his glorious inheritance in the saints.

(Ephesians 1:18)

My hope comes from God's Word.

For everything that was written in the past was written to teach us, so that through endurance and encouragement of the Scriptures we might have hope.

(Romans 15:4)

Hope is not wishful thinking or wanting my desires to be met. My hope is given by God as an assurance that the things I don't see are true, and that the things that will occur in the future are also true.

Now faith is being sure of what we hope for and certain of what we do not see.

(Hebrews 11:1)

But if we hope for what we do not yet have, we wait for it patiently.

(Romans 8:24)

In God's Word hope is also directed at God.

Through him you believe in God, who raised him from the dead and glorified him, and so your faith and hope are in God.

(1 Peter 1:21)

Application

1. What sin do you need to confess today? When will you do it?
2. How or what will you change so that you do not repeat this sin?

A Plan

God has a plan for my life, you say,
And I must work toward it each day.
But how can that be,
That God has a plan for me?
I'm not famous or great, I'm little and small;
But God loves his children, one and all.
So I'll do my best, though I don't understand,
Why God has for me, the perfect plan.
For the plan I will search and try to find,
I'll even ask God to bring it to my mind.
Lord, what is Your plan for me,
In quiet moments He says, "You'll see.
For now, just serve and honor and glorify My name,
Follow My Word; to love Me and others, you don't need
    fame."
I'm humbled by his words so true;
I bow, and, God, I give my life to You.

Blessings: Through the Years

Blessings, August 24, 2008

1. I can stand on the promises of God's Word; it provides me with all I need.
2. God is with me and watching over me.
3. I have taken care of a lot of business stuff.
4. Lunch with Wanda and her granddaughters, Taylor and Sloan. The fellowship and the girls are very entertaining.
5. Bill's call, just to see how I am doing. (Katie is away.)

Blessings, August 24, 2009

Attribute of God: God is my high tower, my strength, my hiding place, and the One whom I trust.

1. I have God's Word in my heart.
2. Safe travel with Shirley to Three Rivers and back home.
3. My beautiful dahlias. Your magnificent creations are a delight. They are purple, red, and white.
4. Time to just sit and watch the hummingbirds at the feeder. So tiny and pretty.
5. ———— is healing and recovering well. You are the Great Healer. (Too personal to describe.)
6. You carry my burden, regarding ———— (Again, too personal to describe.)

My prayer:
Thank You for today, Lord. And I know Your mercy is new every day. You are the Great Healer. And today is a new day for me to start living for You. I know I slipped some living on

vacation, and You have forgiven me. I ask today to be given the strength and power to change. I will use that power. I know what to put off and what to put on. I can, and will, do it. I know You are with me every minute, and it is only You whom I can trust completely. Help me to remain positive and patient this day. To look to others and their needs. And to put aside my selfish desires and self-centeredness. It is my desire to please You, my almighty God.

In Jesus' name I pray. Amen.

Blessings, August 14, 2010

Attribute of God: God's greatest work is His redemption of us.

1. Lunch with Dr. Thomas and ladies from church (nine). Fun, fellowship, and sharing.
2. Dr. Thomas's message: "Where is God in your problem?"
3. We had three people from the community come to workshop. An answered prayer.
4. All the little things I often take for granted—water, electricity, car, sleep, etc., etc.

So many blessings every day, God. You are awesome. God, You are great.

My prayer:

Dear Heavenly Holy Father,

I don't know when Jesus will come; only You do. I could be living in the last days, so I need to be strong, so I can be a tower of strength to others who are drowning in the world around them. I want Your word to dominate my mind, my will, my thoughts, and my emotions. Because I have Your word in my heart, I will not be shaken or easily moved by the things that occur in the world around me. I know I have You, Father, and You are in control of everything. You have placed me in these days, and even if they are the last days, I will live without fear because I have all the promises that are written in Your Word.

I do not fear anything. As I listen to the news and hear all that is happening in the world, I know You will always be here with me—You will never leave me, reject me, or forsake me. I am secure in Your arms. And if Jesus comes during my lifetime, I'll be ready. Thank You, Father, for the peace You have placed in me.

In Jesus' precious name I pray. Amen.

Revisit Memories

In my grief journal I lamented the fact that I had not made enough happy, fun, joyous memories with Bud. On many occasions, I encouraged married couples to make memories a priority. I would tell them that, after someone dies, memories are all that is left.

Today I have discovered another aspect of memories. They do help us remember the person we've lost and recall joyful occasions. But of equal importance is realizing that memories are things we make; if we don't make new memories, we will run out of happy times to recall. Each day, I must work to make memories for others to remember. When my children, grandchildren, family, friends, church family, and others think about me, what will they remember?

I hope they will remember me as a devoted servant of God. That I was totally and completely committed to my Lord and Savior, Jesus Christ. A loving, kind, compassionate wife, mother, MamMaw, friend, and family member who cared about everyone and took care of many. One who always had time to spend with each, to listen attentively and to love unconditionally with all my heart. And most important, that they saw God glorified in all that I did and all that I had.

The questions I must ask myself today are, Am I willing to sacrifice my time and energy to make memories that will last beyond my life? When with others, will I focus on myself, or will I focus on making memories for others to have and keep?

Starting right now, I will commit to making kind and loving memories. To making many happy memories that will bring tears of joy to my loved ones, now and after I am gone.

Dear heavenly Father, please help me to leave behind memories of my love for You and my love of others.

He told us you always have pleasant memories of us and that you long to see us, just as we also long to see you.

(1 Thessalonians 3:6b)

Baby Birds Fly from Nest

August 15, 2010 (two years since Bud passed away)

*B*ud found his wings and flew away to heaven, just as tiny birds fly from the nest.

As his wife, I had loved him. I had cared for and nurtured him through countless medical and physical problems. And then God called him home.

And now my blessed Lord will care for and nature me, until I too fly away to my eternal resting place.

Surely goodness and love shall follow me all the days of my life, and I will dwell in the house of the LORD forever.

(Psalm 23:6)

Isaiah gives a small glimpse of heaven:

No longer will violence be heard in your land, nor ruin or destruction within your borders, but you will call your walls Salvation and your gates Praise.

The sun will no more be your light by day, nor will the brightness of the moon shine on you, for the LORD will be your everlasting light, and your God will be your glory.

Your sun will never set again and your moon will wane no more; the LORD will be your everlasting light, and your days of sorrow will end.

(Isaiah 60:18-20)

Behind the Closed Door

A closed door stands before me;
What lies beyond, I cannot see.
I stare at that closed door;
Open it, God, I want to see more.
I want to see the throne on which you sit,
And see Bud as he kneels before it.
Gently God takes my hand and says to me,
"At this time, there is nothing for you to see;
I want you to serve me with devotion and love.
Bud will be watching you from above;
You love him still, this is true,
And he and I both love you too.
But here on earth is where you must stay,
And wait until I call you home, some glorious day."
Now beyond that door, I know Bud waits
until my work is done; God knows the date.

Cherished Memories

This morning I have spent several hours just looking at cherished old photos and recalling happy memories and some regrets.

One regret is that I did not write down all the memories Bud had shared with me over the years. He fondly recalled memories of his childhood, growing up "down home" in southern Illinois. His colorful descriptions of people and places; nicknames, such as Pancake Patterson, and places like Pickle City and Pond Creek. His grandmother's homestead was on Pond Creek. I made the mistake of calling Pond Creek, Swamp Hollow. I only made that mistake once!

He told me about coming to Michigan and sleeping in Bronson Park his first night; and about his first job, at age seventeen, as a cook at a VA hospital. I do recall many of his experiences in the Navy and working at Douglas Aircraft in California. However, there are so many I don't remember. I did write down a few. I just didn't take the time to listen attentively to him. Looking back, I could have been jotting things down as he shared his life with me. If I had, I could now be walking with him down his memory lane. What joy that would bring to me.

Sometimes I cry when a precious memory comes to mind. Although Bud seldom said it, I know he loved me and cared for me in so many ways.

[AUTHOR'S NOTE: *Though not part of my journal, this is very important! Tell those you love how much you love them, and they will have sweet memories to recall. The more often you tell them, the more happy memories they will have.*]

I remember Bud always called Scott and Teresa by his nicknames for them, Scottie and Squirrel. He had a hard time remembering names, so everyone was either "Jagabog" or "what's his name." I remember his love for kids; he would always give candy and little gifts to them. He loved to farm and just to be outdoors. He enjoyed caring for all our animals—cows, pigs, ducks, geese, chickens, dogs, and even a horse. And he fed and watered my sheep. Each year, he looked forward to deer hunting, often up north. One of my favorite memories is when I went pheasant hunting with him.

There are many more wonderful and pleasant memories that I'll recall as time goes on.

Hope

September 2010

When I walked on the low road, I was fearful. The landscape was so bleak and barren. The road was steep, rocky, and slippery, with deep gorges on each side.

Now I have put my hope in Jesus Christ once more. The presence of God gives me the confidence to pass through those difficult places and circumstances in my life; I have no fear that God will ever desert me.

I must put all my hope in Jesus Christ. I know with certainty that my hope is in My Lord and Savior. I do not put my hope in other people or in material things.

My hope comes only from the Lord, not from: my strength, my intelligence, or favorable circumstances. But from the Lord alone! God is Master of heaven and earth. God alone has the right to promise hope. Only He has the power to keep that promise. My only hope is in Christ.

May the God of hope fill you with all joy and peace as you trust in him, so that you may overflow with hope by the power of the Holy Spirit.

(Romans 15:13)

Low Road/High Road

I traveled the low road, once upon a time,
And the Devil was there, casting out his line.
To snare and trap me with lies and deceit,
Pulling me downward in defeat.
But my God called out to me one day,

"Come with me, I'll show you the way."
And now my feet are planted on the high road,
I'm walking and talking with God, as He carries my load.
He took me from a road so treacherous,
And filled me with hope, joy, and righteousness.
Each day I find God's mercy is new,
His grace is sufficient and his promises true.

A Rainbow

January 2010

I'm walking down a dark path, and up ahead I see a bright light far, far away. I hear a soft, gentle voice behind me saying, "This is the way; walk in it."

Suddenly I'm at a rickety old bridge. Below is a rushing river with white water rapids flowing over huge boulders. There is a troll-like creature hiding beneath the bridge, just waiting to grab me and pull me down into the frigid water.

But shining brightly over the bridge is the most stunning, awe-inspiring rainbow. Each color becomes more brilliant as my eyes fix upon them. I stand spellbound, trying to take it all in.

Colors so dazzling, I have to look away for a moment. The red as red as blood, Jesus' shed blood. Blue, bluer than the bluest of blue skies. Yellow, the brilliant radiant sun. Green, the peaceful pastures. Purple, the royalty of Jesus. White, sins cleansed as white as snow.

Above the rainbow is a powerful, strong arm. It reaches down and gently takes my hand. God lifts me up, and I take a walk upon the rainbow. The surface is so soft, inviting me to skip, hop, and jump. I feel as light as a feather. Peace and calm surround me.

Then the strong arm, with tenderness, sets me firmly on the ground at the other end of the rainbow. I've crossed over that threatening bridge and water.

As I start out, an intense yet soothing light is illuminating my path. God has put before me a peaceful, tranquil scene. Arrays of delicate, multicolored flowers sway back and forth in perfect harmony, as if dancing to a symphonic orchestra. Occasionally a fine mist waters them. I see a road, and I wonder where it will lead and if I should follow it.

Again, that soft gentle voice says, "This is the way; walk in it."

CONNIE SUMMERS

I whisper, "I'm coming, Lord."

Whether you turn to the right or the left, your ears will hear a voice behind you, saying, "This is the way; walk in it."
(Isaiah 30:21)

Brightness Like the Rainbow

Today I have joy in my heart and excitement within me;
Through God's eyes, only sunshine and brightness I see.
My steps are lighter,
My eyes wide open and brighter.
God's Word and His promises, I have heard,
And His light is guiding and leading me onward.

Bible Study Fellowship— Leaders' Meeting

September 2010

Today I start my leadership in Bible Study Fellowship (BSF). I am so excited! BSF has led me into and through several books of the Bible. I have gained knowledge of God's Word from Romans, Matthew, Moses, John, and now Isaiah. Isaiah is leading me into unknown territory: prophecy. I have quoted Isaiah several times in my journals, but I did not read the whole book until last summer.

I know being a leader is a huge responsibility. I am thanking You, Father, for giving me this opportunity to serve You; it is both a privilege and a blessing. Jesus you are the Great Shepherd, and I am asking You to shepherd me as I shepherd my group. I need Your guidance and direction. I pray, dear Lord, that I will be able to follow Your example as I lead my group. To lead them through the lessons by encouraging each of them to be in Your Word daily as they study and complete the lessons. I pray also that each lady will feel comfortable and take an active part in our group discussions, resulting in rich and sweet sharing and learning. Please, Father, equip me to be a compassionate, kind, patient, and understanding leader who leads with love. And may all I do and say be for Your glory.

As I prepare for my first leaders' meeting, I'm very apprehensive and anxious, uncertain as to what to expect. I attended two meetings last spring, but I can't remember much about them. I was very overwhelmed. I hope that isn't an indication of what's to come.

Please, Father, be with me today. Help me to concentrate on all the new information that Debbie presents. You know new situations are always difficult for me. There will be so many experienced leaders in the group, who are very knowledgeable about You and know Your Word so completely. They have Your Word planted firmly in their hearts. I do know, Father, You called me to this ministry. I know You will equip me and be with me in leaders' meeting, as well as in my discussion group. You have not asked me to do more than I am able. But Father, You are stretching me far beyond what I could ever have imagined. (And I thought leading Sparks in AWANA was difficult!)

Well, Father, time to go. Wanda and I will ride together. And I thank You again for Wanda; she has been such an encourager and support person. Once again, I thank You for the wonderful opportunity to serve You, my Lord and Savior.

Anxious:

Do not be anxious about anything, but in everything, by prayer and petition, with thanksgiving, present your requests to God.

(Philippians 4:6)

Equipped:

Equip you with everything good for doing his will, and may he work in us, what is pleasing to him, through Jesus Christ, to whom be glory for ever and ever. Amen.

(Hebrews 13:21)

Serving:

It is the Lord Christ you are serving.

(Colossians 4:24b)

My Best Friend, God

People often tell you to seek a friend to comfort, support, and encourage you in your grief. It is true, a friend can play an important part when you are grieving.

There is comfort that comes from sharing difficulties with a friend, but sometimes this comfort is only temporary. This may leave you wanting more. I am not saying a friend cannot give comfort. A close friend can, at times, comfort and encourage you. Many times during my grieving, I needed a friend.

However there is one true friend who is always there to comfort, encourage and love you.

That friend is God.

Only God can give you immediate, ongoing, and lasting comfort, because God is available 24/7. It is never too early in the morning or too late at night. And it doesn't matter where you are; God will always hear you.

God listens attentively to whatever you want to share. You are very important to God. He asks only that you seek Him, and that you have a sincere desire to talk with Him.

I love those who love me, and those who seek me, find me.
(Proverbs 8:17)

Showers

Today I am going to take a walk in the woods. I want to once again see God's wonderful, marvelous creations.

As I walk, I feel a few raindrops on my head. I know this will not be a hard, pelting rain. God is sending a gentle refreshing shower. There is no need for an umbrella. I won't get wet, for this is a glorious heavenly shower.

Each drop is showering me with blessings, encouragement, comfort, joy, peace, and revival for my weary soul. The drops become a downpour of God's unconditional love.

Thank You, Father, for showers.

I will bless them and the places surrounding my hill, I will send down showers in season; there will be showers of blessing.

(Ezekiel 34:26)

More Junk Emptied

This morning I am putting a whole bushel of junk into my junk bag. Junk I have let accumulate in my heart and mind. This junk is just too heavy and too toxic for me to carry any longer.

First to go into the junk bag are all those old hurts from the past. I'm choosing not to remember any of them. In go the misunderstandings, the feelings of rejection, the judging of motives, the critical words spoken to me, my feelings of inadequacy, my sad memories, my out-of-control emotions, and anything that leads to disobedience to my God.

> You were taught, with regard to your former way of life, to put off your old self, which is being corrupted by deceitful desires; and to put on the new self, created to be like God in true righteousness and holiness.
>
> (Ephesians 4:22, 24)

All that negativity is now in the junk bag. I will never have to carry any of it ever again.

Lord, thank You for helping me to empty all that junk from my heart and mind. I feel so much lighter and newer. Please help me to be aware when junk comes into my mind, and to get rid of it immediately, so it does not start to accumulate again.

In place of the junk, I am filling my mind with the attributes of God. I started this list of attributes a long time ago and continue to add to it: God is the divine creator.

God created everything that exists on earth and in Heaven.

God sustains all of His creation.

God is unchangeable. What He says He will do, He does.

God is all powerful, all knowing, and always present.

God is everywhere at the same time.
God is truth and His Word is truth.
God is, has always been, and always will be.
God is Holy and Righteous.
God is love. His love is unconditional and endures forever.
God is the alpha and omega, the beginning and the end.
God is merciful; His mercies are new every day.
God's grace is sufficient, and it is by His grace I was saved and not of deeds.
God is carrier of my burdens.
God is the Trinity: the Father, Son, and Holy Spirit.
God is my provider, reformer, encourager, supporter, director, leader, comforter, and protector.
God is the giver of all blessings.
God is my daily bread and my fountain of living water.

Little Ellie

About a year and a half after Bud passed away, my great-niece, Laura, had a miscarriage. Laura and her husband, Dustin—as well as both their families—were devastated.

Laura sat down with her daughter, Ellie, then four years old, to tell her about losing the baby.

Laura could hardly hold back the tears as she told Ellie, "Mama is not going to have a baby. The baby died in Mama's stomach."

Ellie could see how sad her mama was. Her reply was, "Don't cry, Mama. The baby is in heaven, and Uncle Bud is holding her in his arms."

What faith and belief from a small child.

What an amazing God! He used little Ellie to bring comfort to her mama.

In 2011 God blessed this family with a precious, healthy baby girl.

God is the Great I Am

God the creator
God the maker
God of light
God of might
God the potter
God of living water
God supreme
God unseen
God the Great King
God ruler of everything
God of integrity
God of equality
God divine
God of mine
God of salvation
God of revelation
God of Jews
God of Gentiles, too
God of earth
God of the universe
God sustainer of all the land
God creator of woman and man
God the true God
God who rules with a strong rod
God of Holiness
God of Righteousness

"I am the LORD, and there is no other; apart from me
there is no God."
(Isaiah 45:5a)

Mountains and Valleys

God has smoothed the mountains of my life and filled in the valleys.
He has me walking on a smooth straight path which is joyful,
exciting, busy, and fulfilling.

My steps have held to your paths; my feet have not slipped.
(Psalm 17:5)

All of a sudden I put up detour signs for myself.
I always have a choice to continue on God's path, which can become
bumpy and rough at times, or take the detour, which will definitely
lead to destruction.
Foolishly, I often follow detour signs that lead me into the dark
unknown.

A prudent man sees danger and takes refuge, but the simple
keep going and suffer for it.
(Proverbs 22:3)

Stern discipline awaits him who leaves the path.
(Proverbs 15:10a)

When I follow God's path, regardless of the bumps and roughness, God
will always be there. He will use his mighty right hand as a bulldozer,
making the path ahead of me smooth and straight.

The path of the righteous is level;
O upright One, you make the way of the
righteous smooth.
(Isaiah 26:7)

243

Right now, dear Lord, I am choosing Your smooth straight path, with whatever bumps You place in my way. Whatever I encounter on Your path will be for my good and Your glory. You will not let me fall off Your path again.

They will come weeping; they will pray and as I bring them back, I will lead them beside streams of water on a level path where they will not stumble.

(Jeremiah 31:9a)

Walking in obedience to Your Word will keep me on Your path of righteousness. You know what I need, where I am going, and how I will get there.

I guide you in the way of wisdom and lead you along straight paths.

(Proverbs 4:11)

Show me your ways, O LORD, teach me your paths.

(Psalm 25:4)

Dear Lord and Savior, only You can get me to my final destination safely. My arrival will be a joyous glorious celebration.

You have made known to me the path of life; you will fill me with joy in your presence, with eternal pleasures at your right hand.

(Psalm 16:11)

Application

1. What mountain are you trying to climb which seems impossible? Who will you call on for help?

2. Are you stuck in a valley? Do you see any way out? What is that way?

3. Do you always expect a smooth, straight path, with no bumps or roughness? Whom or what do you turn to when a detour leads you astray? A friend? Alcohol? Shopping? Eating? Television? Gambling? God? God's Word? What are you seeking as you turn to these?

Glenn and Ruthie

October 2010

Glenn and Ruthie came to supper last night. Glenn has shown such kindness to me since Bud's death; of course, Ruthie too is very caring. Glenn surprises me all the time. He always spends time listening to me.

And Ruthie told me Glenn is often the one who prompts their visits and phone calls. Another surprise last night: Glenn asked if he could read what I had written in my book, even though it isn't complete. He'd only read about a third of the pages when it was time for supper. He asked me what has made the second year harder than the first. This morning I've been thinking about this. I'm not really sure. But I think subconsciously I bought into those comments from people when Bud died. I think I really thought a year was enough time and I should be back to normal. (*Have I ever been normal? What's normal?*) Why did I think grief knew the calendar? "Okay," says grief, "it's been 364 days, and tomorrow I am out of here."

I do know that my life with Bud can never be again. For forty-six years we were a couple, and now I am a "one," a "single." Time will never change that; only I can. With the help of the Holy Spirit I can change from being one to being two, three, four, or more—but only by reaching out to others.

I will continue to intertwine my life with many people. To share precious time with special people. To be there when they need a friend and when they want a friend.

Forget the former things; do not dwell on the past.
(Isaiah 43:18)

God's Blessings

Thank You, heavenly holy Father, for Your many blessings:

For eyes to see the beautiful, magnificent sunset last night. A picture-perfect masterpiece.

For ears to hear Your many, many birds singing each day.

For a nose to smell the sweet fragrance of blooming flowers in my garden.

For hands to feel the softness of my fluffy cat.

For feet to carry me through the woods, with trees displaying dazzling multicolored leaves.

For a mouth to taste the sweetness of fresh strawberries in the spring and ripe tomatoes in the summer.

For a brain to read, learn, and understand Your Word.

For a body filled with the Holy Spirit.

For a heart filled with love for You and for others.

For eternal life, as it was by Your grace that I was saved, not by my own works.

And I will live with You in Your kingdom forever and ever.

A Discovery

October 2010

As I was reading and studying Philippians, chapter 4, verse 7, I found a note beside the previous verse. The note was dated February 21, 2008, and it read, "That's me now." The verse begins with these words:

Do not be anxious about anything

(Philippians 4:6)

That same day, I wrote in my journal that I have never been a worrier. My mom and her sisters worried about everything. We used to joke that Mom worried because she didn't have anything to worry about. Today I can again say, "That's me now." However, this passage means much more to me than the simple instruction to just not worry. I've learned a lot from verse 6 by meditating on it. My anxiety and worries put undue stress on me. They also indicate that I am not trusting in God. I am not relying on His wisdom, His sovereignty, or His power.

I would like you to be free from concern.

(1 Corinthians 7:32a)

God wants me to be free from anxiety, stress, and personal/worldly concerns.

So then, banish anxiety from your heart and cast off the troubles of your body.

(Ecclesiastes 11:10a)

God is always aware of my situation.

I am concerned about their suffering.
(Exodus 5:7b)

God's Word tells me what my response should be.

And when they heard that the LORD was concerned about them and had seen their misery, they bowed down and worshipped.
(Exodus 4:31b)

Here is the end of verse 6:

[B]ut in everything, by prayer and petition, with thanksgiving, present your requests to God.
(Philippians 4:6)

Prayer and petition:

So I turned to the LORD God and pleaded with him in prayer and petition.
(Daniel 9:3a)

Now, our God, hear the prayers and petitions of your servant.
(Daniel 9:17a)

Thanksgiving:

[T]hat my heart may sing to you and not be silent.
O LORD, my God, I will give thanks forever.
(Psalm 30:12)

Verse 6 flows naturally into verse 7:

And the peace of God, which transcends all understanding, will guard your hearts and your minds in Christ Jesus.
(Philippians 4:7)

God gives me an inner calm. He frees my mind from anxiety, stress, doubt, fear, troublesome thoughts, and uncontrollable emotions. I really can't comprehend how God does this, because outside of me the same problems, struggles, and difficult situations still exist. I just know that when I trust in and rely on God, He protects and guards my heart and mind.

When anxiety and stress starts to creep into my life and mind, I need to immediately go to God in prayer.

Listen to my prayer, O God, do not ignore my plea; hear me
and answer me.
My thoughts trouble me and I am distraught.
(Psalm 55:1-2)

God hears and answers my prayers.
I am peaceful, untroubled, and content because I am united with
my Lord and Savior, Jesus Christ.

The LORD gives strength to his people; the LORD blesses his
people with peace.
(Psalm 29:11)

Application

1. What do you worry about? Job? Kids? Weather? Your appearance? Other people?
2. What do you do when worry or anxiety becomes too much to deal with? Who do you go to? Friend? Mother/Father? Pastor? God? Why do you go to that person?

A Temporary Storm

November 2010

My mind is screaming at me, *Don't be sad and gloomy tonight. Think about some happy, happy memories.* I will. I'll take a walk with Bud. We will hold hands as we walk through the woods behind our house. We will make plans to dig that pond Bud has wanted for so long. Or plan our trip to Illinois; the family will be very happy to see us. The trees are so pretty—leaves of red, orange, and yellow. Our favorite time of the year. *Remember this, remember this.* So many happy memories are floating around in my mind, making me dizzy.

But a nice kind of dizzy.

In the distance I see a flash of lightning, almost like a warning. Dark, menacing clouds begin to hover over my head. A drizzle of rain starts falling—suddenly becoming a cloudburst, pelting me with huge raindrops. Lightning blazes across my eyes, almost blinding me. The thunder rumbles and roars in my head, causing an unrelenting headache. The force of the bitter wind is so great, I just can't stand up against it. *No! No! No! No!* Not this time. I will not give in to this violent, unpredictable storm. Not again.

I need You, God. I'm searching, Lord; help me. I can see Your guiding light, like a beacon, leading me out of this raging turbulence of uncontrollable debilitating emotions. Lord, Your mighty power has stopped this unstoppable storm in my mind.

I am safe, warm and dry, with You my Lord, my Comforter and Savior.

I open my Bible:

Jesus replied, "You are in error because you do not know the Scriptures or the power of God." (Matthew 22:29)

Lesson

Jesus was talking to the Sadducees. But I feel the rebuke also. And it hurts. I repeatedly ask God to lead me to the Scriptures I need. And once again, He does. Now I must ask myself, in all my reading and studying, do I fully understand that passage? It is not enough to read, or even memorize a verse, if I do not comprehend the meaning. Dear Lord, a deeper understanding is what I'm seeking.

Lift your eyes and look to the heavens:
Who created all these?
He who brings out the starry host one by one, and calls each by name.
Because of his great power and mighty strength, not one of them is missing.

(Isaiah 40:26)

Lesson

God's power and strength last forever. He never gets tired or weary. He is always available to help and to listen. His strength and power are my strength and power.

When I see that storm start to brew in my mind or my life, when I feel I can't move, I can always call on God for strength. Because He has the power to control all nature and to keep the universe going, He certainly has the power to keep me going. (In the right direction!)

Do you not know?
Have you never heard?
The LORD is the everlasting God,
the Creator of the ends of the earth.
He will not grow tired or weary,
and his understanding no one can fathom.
He gives strength to the weary,
and increases the power of the weak.
Even youths grow tired and weary,
and young men stumble and fall;
but those who hope in the LORD

will renew their strength

They will soar high on wings like eagles;

they will run and not grow weary,

they will walk and not be faint.

(Isaiah 40:28-31)

Lesson

God expects and wants me to trust in Him for everything. He will always be there when I need Him. I must cling to the promises in His Word, knowing He will fulfill each promise. He will provide the strength I need for any trial, problem, situation, difficulty, or storm that comes my way. I once thought that all I had to do was ask for strength, and it would be given. Of course, I do need to ask for strength, but then I must make a conscious effort to use that strength and power. The Holy Spirit gives it so freely to me.

My prayer:

God, I know I am weak and without the power to overcome the unpredictable storms that continue to blow into my mind, causing fear and discouragement. I know You are in control, and I'm asking for strength to take each debilitating thought to You, immediately. I have Your promise that You will give me victory over these recurring, destroying thoughts and feelings. My complete trust is in You.

Application

1. Is there a circumstance (storm) in your life that has knocked you off your feet? That you have not been able to handle by yourself? Who or what have you turned to? Friends? Family? Alcohol? Shopping? Something else?

2. When have you tried to solve problems in your own strength? When have you asked God for strength? How did you use that strength? What was the result?

3. What is your understanding of complete trust in God? Do you trust in God for everything? What evidence, in your life, displays this complete trust?

Meaningful Journal Entry

November 2010

*I*t's hard to believe, but I found this entry today. I have come back to where I was two and a half years ago.

Journal Entry, April 5, 2008

Yesterday was a great day for me. I spent about an hour talking to God. And so many things became clear to me. Bud coughed up blood again (third time in two days). I just gave it to God, saying, "You are in control, not me. Whatever happens, or doesn't happen, it will be Your will."

God, that was a brief summary of what we talked about yesterday. As I finished talking to You, I felt a peace I've never felt before. A deeper peace. God, You led me to make the necessary phone calls. And there I left it in Your hands.

My thoughts are positive: I have Jesus holding me up and God smiling down on me.

Here I am. I'm floating on a clear, clean river, with Jesus standing beside me, holding me up. God is smiling down upon us. Sometimes the fish nibble or take a deep bite out of me. But Jesus heals the wound quickly and keeps me afloat.

I see a bend in the river. I do not fear what is beyond that bend, for I know whatever is there is in God's control, not mine. And whatever happens is by His will and for my good.

Down deep at the bottom of that river are darkness, muck, and evil things. And I know, at times, I may sink down into that muck. But by God's grace and mercy I will not get stuck there.

God will forgive me and bring me to the top of the river, into the brightness where Jesus is waiting with open arms.

Morning and Night

Nearing the first of December, it takes morning a little longer to get here. I know it will arrive in God's time and in His way. I wonder if the sun will creep slowly over the horizon until its full golden radiance is seen. Or if it will send out spikes of brilliant red to announce it is coming. Perhaps there will suddenly be glorious shades of pink and red across the sky. Or the clouds may hide the sun, and the dawn will arrive clothed in gray.

It is difficult to know when evening has passed into night. The sky has been filled with dark clouds all day. The sun has chosen to hide away, perhaps to get some much needed rest. Now the clock tells me it is getting late. Yet the stars have not appeared, and the moon can't be seen.

I am at peace with this extreme darkness outside. I know God is in control, and tomorrow He will again make the day and evening as He desires: bright, dark, or in between. And each will come according to His schedule. God is the divine Creator.

"It is I who made the earth
and created mankind upon it.
My own hands stretched out the heavens;
I marshaled their starry hosts."

(Isaiah 45:12)

Where Is Jesus?

December is a week away. Yet the stores are filled with so many worldly things of Christmas. Santa Clauses, alive or stuffed; stockings, large and small; holiday trees; gingerbread men; holly; mistletoe; animated reindeer playing "Jingle Bells"; snow globes displaying Santa's workshop; advertisements enticing us to buy more and more; signs that read, "Happy Holidays".

Where is peace on earth and goodwill toward men? Where is Merry Christmas? Where is Jesus?

Jesus is where His Word tells us. He sits on the throne at the right hand of God. He resides in our hearts. He is in the midst of our troubles and struggles. He is walking and talking with us moment by moment. He is in the garden. He is in our churches and in our homes. He is riding with as we travel, keeping us safe. He is a guest at our tables, providing our food. He is listening and answering our prayers. He is blessing us. He is forgiving our sins and trespasses. He is in the songs we sing: "Away in the Manger" and "Silent Night". He is in the eyes of the children as they hear about Jesus' birth. He is in the stars, the moon, the sun, the rain, and snow.

He is watching over all His creation and His beloved children. And He is patiently waiting for His lost children to come to Him. Yes, Jesus is everywhere. And I rejoice in Him this Christmas season. I bow my head and pray for peace and for a Jesus-centered Christmas for all.

[A]nd she gave birth to her firstborn, a son. She wrapped him in cloths and placed him in a manger, because there was no room for them in the inn.

(Luke 2:7)

But the angel said to them, "Do not be afraid. I bring you good news of great joy that will be for all the people. Today in the town of David a Savior has been born to you; he is Christ the Lord. This will be a sign to you: You will find a baby wrapped in cloths and laying in a manger."

(Luke 2:10-12)

I Love Knitting

December 2010

I finished my scarf. Thank You, Lord, for helping me to concentrate. I know my mind is improving and starting to function a little better. The scarf isn't much, but it is pretty, very fuzzy and very practical. My wandering mind takes me back to last year, when I tried to knit a baby sweater. How I tangled the yarn. Yesterday I untangled it so I can use it again.

It's kind of like Jesus is untangling the mess I've made of my life. And he is using me again. All I had to do was pray and ask him to untangle all those messed up synapses that cause confused thoughts in my brain. To eliminate the short-circuited ones and connect my thought processes to God and His Word.

Therefore, holy brothers, who share in the heavenly calling,
fix your thoughts on Jesus, the apostle and high priest whom
we confess.
(Hebrews 3:1)

Christmas 2010

I bought dozens of tiny angel ornaments made of clay. On each, I will write the name of family and friends who have passed away.

Next year I will have a memory tree. As I hang each angel on the tree, I will recall a special memory of that person.

Winter Wonderland

January 2011

Lord, I'm off to shovel the snow You so generously deposited on my driveway last night.

Once outside, I see the very hard work that lies ahead for me; but I also see Your marvelous masterpiece of beauty and splendor.

You have, as always, provided for me. You have clothed me in extra-warm winter attire, heavy socks and high boots. A new snow shovel, how grand! You give me strength and physical ability to shovel six inches of snow from a very large area. Also, the motivation to persevere till the job is completed. My physical exercise in your winter wonderland.

I marvel at the tiny winter birds, perfectly lined up on the telephone wire, chirping so sweetly. The trees are at rest, awaiting the arrival of spring. My flowers, asleep under your blanket of snow. The crisscrossing hoofprints of deer, as they romp and play, momentarily free from the bushes that protect them. Swirling tiny lines in the snow, made by little scurrying critters out for an afternoon of fun.

The most precious thing to me is the quiet time I have with You, alone in piles of snow, with Your beauty and majesty surrounding me. Even the wind has settled down for a little while. All is quiet and peaceful in this part of your earth.

There is joy in my heart as I finish; a job well done.

It is late afternoon; in the sky is the most awe-inspiring sight. Your sun is setting in the western sky and transforming it into brilliant hues, gorgeous reds and pinks. You have painted the perfect picture for me to end my day. Thank You, Father.

I stand spellbound, watching the sunset, as a truck pulls into my driveway. A neighbor has come to plow out my drive. He just slowly backs away. Your timing is always perfect, Lord.

The warmth of my house greets me, and a cup of tea beckons. Sipping my tea and reflecting on the day, I glance out the window. Large snowflakes are gracefully and rapidly tumbling down to the ground. I smile. God, You are full of surprises, and You have a sense of humor. I love You and thank You for this blessed day.

God has a purpose for the snow, extreme, low temperatures, and harsh winters. I don't know His purpose, but I accept this as God's will.

Reasons to Be Thankful for Snow

1. It may keep someone home who would not be safe if out in the cold.
2. It is preparing me to look ahead to spring with delightful anticipation.
3. It gives me an opportunity to do my strengthening exercises by shoveling snow.
4. I am being obedient to God when I go out and continue to serve Him, regardless of weather.
5. It gives me extra time to study God's Word.
6. The sunshine today is so appreciated, and I thank God.
7. Snow is amazing: its brightness, as well as the way that such tiny flakes can create gigantic piles of snow.
8. God clearly reveals himself as the divine Creator.
9. Maybe the lakes and rivers will need the water this spring.
10. The snow protects my perennial flowers.
11. Most important, I am reminded that God is in control.

Medical and Spiritual Checkups

February 2011

Another year has passed, and another annual physical exam has been completed. Once again, God has blessed me with excellent health. Now I am ready for my annual spiritual checkup.

In prayer, I go to the Great Physician. God, please, give me a complete spiritual evaluation and perform the necessary restoration. I want to be assured that my attitude, actions, and thoughts are the ones You desire of me. To have the confidence that all I do is for Your glory.

Request for Heart Scan

"'I the LORD search the heart and examine the mind, to reward a man according to his conduct, according to what his deeds deserve.'"

(Jeremiah 17:10)

A spiritual heart scan can be compared to a CAT scan of the brain, used to detect tumors. A heart scan can detect any hidden sin, which could, if left unchecked and untreated, lead to disastrous consequences.

Results of Heart Scan

O LORD, you have searched me
and you know me.
You know when I sit and when I rise;
you perceive my thoughts from afar.
You discern my going out and my lying down;
you are familiar with all my ways.

(Psalm 139:1-3)

God knows everything there is to know about me. He even knows the number of hairs on my head. (So You know, Lord, they are getting pretty thin!)

And even the very hairs of your head are all numbered.
(Matthew 10:30)

Consultation

Although not the results I had hoped for, they were not a surprise. I know I am a sinner who sins against my almighty God. I know I must confess and repent of my sins each day.

If we confess our sins, he is faithful and just and will forgive us our sins and purify us from all unrighteousness.
(1 John 1:9)

Follow-up

To always trust in God, safe in the knowledge that He is always with me. He is omnipresent (present everywhere and at all times.) He knows and sees everything I do, everything I say, and everything I think.

Where can I go from your Spirit?
Where can I flee from your presence?
(Psalm 139:7)

Prescription

Receive comforting reassurance. No matter what I do or where I go, I will never be away from God's loving, faithful care.

For the LORD is good and his love endures forever; his faithfulness continues through all generations.
(Psalm 100:5)

GRIEVING FOR THE GLORY OF GOD

Praise God always.

I will praise you, O LORD, with all my heart;
I will tell of your wonders.
I will be glad and rejoice in you;
I will sing praise to your name, O Most High.
(Psalm 9:1-2)

Lung Function Test: Normal

Although an adequate exchange of oxygen is wonderful news, there is another type of exchange to be considered: negative versus positive thinking.

Treatment

Take a deep, deep breath. Hold for a minute, as the air is expelled, visualize it carrying all those harmful, sinful, unhealthy, negative thoughts, and behaviors out of me.

Inhale the pure, clean Word of God. Let His Word flow into me and fill my heart and mind with His love, His truths, and His promises.

Follow-up

I will rejoice with each lifesaving breath God has given me.

And he is not served by human hands, as if he needed anything, because he himself gives men life and breath and everything else.
(Acts 17:25)

The LORD God formed the man from dust of the ground and breathed into his nostrils the breath of life, and the man became a living being.
(Genesis 2:7)

I will praise God always.

Let everything that has breath praise the LORD.
Praise the LORD.

(Psalm 150:6)

Icy Masterpiece

February 2011

Last night, just before bedtime, the snow changed to freezing rain. I awoke at 3:00 a.m. to a red blinking light, my clock alerting me to a disruption in electricity. I reset all the blinking clocks and returned to bed, only to awake at 5:30 a.m. to find the clock blinking once again. As I made my way to the kitchen to make coffee, I noticed that there was no readout on the thermostat. Having no success in restarting the furnace, I called for help.

Now I'm bundled up with a heavy throw across my lap, waiting for the repairman. God, thank You, for my electricity being on now after going off three different times, and please keep the repairman safe as he travels today.

All my thoughts of being cold and uncomfortable are forgotten as I look out the window.

God has painted a beautiful, majestic, icy landscape. Ice covers the trees completely, causing them to glisten, as if sprinkled with glitter. God must have been working all night, polishing each tree to a dazzling, sparkling shine. As the wind gently moves the branches, there is a crackling noise like that of a log burning in a fireplace. God, I thank You for creating beauty beyond compare. You are the divine Creator.

> He spreads the snow like wool
> and scatters the frost like ashes.
> He hurls down his hail like pebbles.
> Who can withstand his icy blast?
> He sends his word and melts them;
> he stirs up his breezes, and the waters flow.
> (Psalm 147:16-18)

Pastor's Sermon, March 20, 2011

March 21, 2011

Good morning, Sweet Jesus. What a difference in the way I feel this morning. I am joyful, peaceful, and contented. My life is great, with an abundance of blessings. I'm thankful for every day, even though some are not so smooth. I know I have You every second of every day—watching and providing for me. What a comfort!

I've reviewed Pastor's sermon on Genesis chapter 22, verses 1 through 19.

He talked about the long journey to the cross and how difficult it was for both the Father and the Son. I remember how Isaiah graphically described the suffering of Jesus in chapter 52.

Dear Lord, Jesus' journey has caused me to think and meditate on His sacrifice on the cross for me.

My journey has been easy; the pain minimal. Forgive me for the times I complained and felt sorry for myself. May I never forget how Jesus suffered and paid the penalty for my sin.

Pastor also listed three lessons about faith:

1. Faith obeys completely the Word of God.
2. Faith surrenders to the best of God, holding nothing back.
3. Faith waits on the Lord to provide all one needs.

(But God often does not provide until a personal sacrifice has been made.)

I am writing these lessons about faith in the front of my journal, so I can review them often.

Holy Spirit

Spring 2011

With the Holy Spirit leading me, I don't have to tell myself what to do. All those things I thought were so important are not. Now I pray for guidance, and I follow the Holy Spirit's leading.

Yesterday, as I followed His directions, He filled my heart to overflowing with love. After a twenty-three-year painful separation, I was led to comfort and encourage a grieving person by giving my unconditional love. God's mighty strength and power tore down that rigid barrier.

[AUTHOR'S NOTE: *I have chosen not to include the situation (or the person) in which the barrier was torn down.*]

His divine power has given us everything we need for life
and godliness through our knowledge of him who called us
by his own glory and goodness.
(2 Peter 1:3)

My heart is so joyous; my soul so peaceful.

How Great Thou Art, Sovereign Lord!

The peace of God's grace and mercy are within me. So many times this week God has answered my prayers (once immediately).

I don't know why I find that so amazing. After all, He is an amazing God, supreme and lifted above all.

Mathematical Equation

Knowledge of God

Oh, the depth of the riches of the wisdom and knowledge of God!

(Romans 11:33a)

PLUS (+)

God's Promises

Through these he has given us his very great and precious promises, so that through them you may participate in the divine nature and escape the corruption in the world caused by evil desires.

(2 Peter 1:4)

PLUS (+)

Faith

Consequently, faith comes from hearing this message and the message is heard through the Word of Christ.

(Romans 10:17)

PLUS (+)

Goodness + Self-Control + Perseverance + Godliness + Brotherly Kindness + Love:

> For this very reason, make every effort to add to your faith goodness; and to goodness, knowledge; and to knowledge, self-control; and to self-control, perseverance; and to perseverance, godliness; and to godliness, brotherly kindness; and to brotherly kindness, love.
>
> (2 Peter 1:5-7)

EQUALS (=)

A Welcome to God's Kingdom

> And you will receive a rich welcome into the eternal kingdom of our Lord and Savior Jesus Chris
>
> (2 Peter 1:11)

A Broken Heart Healed

$\mathcal{W}$hat a great day! Although today may seem like every other day, I know it will be different in many ways. For each day has its share of new exciting things, as well as the routine things. Today is a mysterious day, a day unknown to me. A day God has perfectly planned for me to walk through and to finish strong at the end.

I'm anxiously waiting to see where God will lead me. I am now walking the path He has made straight for me. Although there are occasional valleys and mountains, my path always leads to Him.

I am no longer afraid of stumbling or falling, for God is there to catch me and to pick me up. As I see those dreaded detour signs, I know it is Satan who put them in my way. Satan's greatest desire is to lure me away from my almighty God. In giant bold letters, his sign reads: "Come, this is the way to a carefree, fun life. Everything here is wonderful and lovely. No pain or hurt. You will always be happy, so come."

I am not deceived. God desires me to continue on His path, the path of righteousness. It will, at times, become steep, bumpy, and muddy, with many struggles and even some unhappy situations.

However, I am not worried. God has assured me this is the best and only way to travel, and the only way to reach my final destination. God, I am willing to walk and even run along Your path. I will gladly follow You; lead on.

You have ended my grieving journey. You have guided and led me though a wonderful spiritual journey. You have mended my broken heart. I see it as a miracle, which it is. I am still in awe of how You always know what each of us needs, and Your timing is always perfect. I don't know why I let myself become so unhappy, why I struggled so hard. I just had never felt a pain as devastating as I felt when Bud died. I really didn't know what to do, what not to do, or how to do it. I just did what I thought was best, and that was to work, work, work.

I had to get everything done quickly. Although I wrote about being selfish and self-centered, which I was, my main objective was to get a perceived mess cleaned up. I thought grieving was for wimps.

Each day became just another day to work all day long and to cry all evening. I welcomed it. The exhaustion from hard work and uncontrollable crying let me fall into bed and sleep away the pain. (Now I know God, it was You who gave me the needed rest as I prayed each night.)

God, occasionally I would pray and read Your Word, but most of the time, I was going it alone without You. How amazing are Your mercy and grace. Now I can picture You watching and waiting, as I went down that deserted path alone. Of course, I was never alone; You knew each step I would take, every thought I would have, and everything I would try to do.

Although I frequently did not acknowledge You, You were always patiently waiting. You know the end from the beginning. When it was Your perfect time, You took my hand, and with Your mighty right arm, You lifted me up and into Your arms once more. You called Your lost sheep back to You, and You welcomed me as a shepherd welcomes back his sheep that have strayed. I am once more safe in Your everlasting arms.

It took me awhile to understand and appreciate the marvelous healing You were bringing about in my heart. I now know that the suffering and hopelessness I felt were part of Your perfect plan for me. You showed me that I can do nothing on my own, and all I do and all I have is through Your awesome power and strength. Your mercy healed me; Your grace forgave me; Your loving watch care protected me as You provided for my every need; and Your inspiring Word led me back to You.

And then you lead me back to read, study, and understand Your Word—the truths and promises.

Your Word Tells Me To
Be obedient to Your Word.
Cherish family and friends.
Love my church family.
Attend and learn from Bible Study Fellowship.
Practice daily devotions.

Say my prayers (both daily and spontaneously).
Spend quiet time with you.
Serve others and Your church.
Make time for fun and enjoyment.
Embrace joy, peace, and contentment.

My greatest blessing is You, my holy Father. Through Your Word I was taught to completely and totally trust in You and You alone. You're in control of everything and every person. My faith is strong, and my only desire is to please You, Father.

I kneel on my knees and humbly praise You, my beloved Lord and Savior. All glory is Yours forever and ever. Amen.

[T]o the only God, our Savior be glory, majesty, power and authority, through Jesus Christ our Lord, before all ages, now and forevermore!

Amen

(Jude 1:25)

End of Spiritual Journey

It is summertime, 2011. Although there is so much more I would like to share, I must end this book.

However, my spiritual journey will continue until I am in heaven with my precious Lord, Jesus Christ.

Looking back through the pages of both my grieving and spiritual journeys, I see how far I have come and how far I still have to go. However, now I am standing on a firm foundation, a solid rock.

As I think back, I know I lost my way and separated myself from God at times. My loving, heavenly Father never abandoned me. He knew when it was time for me to move forward, when it was time for my healing to start. He led me to His Word once more; into the learning, the promises, and the truths that I had let slip from my mind and heart.

I hung on tight to God's hand throughout my spiritual journey as I recalled the truths and promises of His Word. The truth of God's greatness and majesty is overwhelming. His promises are so awesome and reliable. His inspired Word is without flaw or error. He is my perfect almighty God, beautiful and desirous. I can always depend on God; what he says He will do, He does.

God is always available to listen to me. He hears my prayers and answers them in His way and in His time. His ways are mysterious ways, and they are not my ways. His timing is always perfect. He guides my footsteps and makes my path straight. He catches me when I stumble, and He picks me up if I fall. He is my strength and my power. He is the potter, and I am the clay. I am weak, but He is strong; He is my strength.

I can fellowship with him, moment by moment, anytime and anywhere. He knows my coming and my going, my needs and my desires. He supplies all my needs and my desires according to his will. He carries my burdens. His burdens are light, and His yoke is easy to bear. When I am weary and heavily laden, I come to him, and He gives me rest.

He gives me peace that transcends all understanding. He is my rock and my fortress, my refuge and sanctuary. He is my provider; all that I have He has provided, and all that I have belongs to Him. He is my protector; He protects me from harm.

He is my daily bread and my fountain of living water; I am never hungry or thirsty. He will never leave me, forsake me, or reject me. He is my joy, my peace, and my contentment.

You have made known to me the path of life; you will fill me with joy in your presence, with eternal pleasures at your right hand.

(Psalm 16:11)

Conclusion

God always provides what I need, when I need it. He knows the end from the beginning. He knows how to intertwine the circumstances and experiences of my life in order to deepen my trust in Him and strengthen me for the future.

What plans does God have for my future? I have no way of knowing. But God does. I know He will carry out His plans. I will be ready to follow his plans.

"I know that you can do all things; no plan of yours can be thwarted."

(Job 42:2)

"What I have said, that I will bring about;
What I have planned, that I will do."

(Isaiah 46:11b)

Commit to the LORD whatever you do,
And your plans will succeed.

(Proverbs 16:3)

My hope for the future lies in my faith and belief in Jesus Christ, my Lord and Savior.

But Jesus remained silent.

The high priest said to him, "I change you under oath by the living God: Tell us if you are the Christ, the Son of God."

"Yes, it is as you say," Jesus replied. "But I say to all of you: In the future you will see the Son of Man sitting at the right hand of the Mighty One and coming on the clouds of heaven."

(Matthew 26:63-64)

Part VII

Additional Information

You, the Grieving Person

Right now it may seem as if you will never get through this difficult time in your life. My heart goes out to all of you who are grieving the loss of a spouse. I wish I could promise that what you are about to read will take away your pain. I cannot promise you that. You may find that the pain never completely goes away. My hope is that you will discover what you can do to help yourself heal, in addition to the healing that comes from the help you receive from others.

Through God's Word, your grieving heart will find all the help and hope needed to begin healing. Within the pages of the Bible are words of comfort, support, and encouragement which will strengthen and renew you. God is the Great Physician. There is nothing He cannot do.

You will grieve, but your grief will turn to joy.
(John 16:20b)

This probably seems impossible to believe right now, but God knows your suffering, and He feels your pain.

[A]nd I am concerned by their suffering.
(Exodus 3:7b)

Believe and trust in Him. He knows what lies ahead, and He has promised to be with you through it all.

And we know in all things God works for the good of those who love him, who have been called according to his purpose.
(Romans 8:28)

You have just suffered a great loss in your life: the death of your husband or wife. Death of a spouse is deeply emotional and stunningly final. It shakes you to your very core. It was not part of God's original plan for us.

Each of you is at a different stage of grief. Regardless of where you are, however, there is hope. As you read, you will find hope, peace, and joy which will encourage and support you as you move through your grief. The Divine Healer is just waiting for you; He wants to heal your broken heart.

He heals the brokenhearted and binds up their wounds.
(Psalm 147:3)

During this time of grief, you may not understand yourself or why you think and/or act the way you do. Your speech and behaviors may be very different from what they used to be. When you feel lonely and don't understand yourself, remember that God understands.

Great is our Lord and mighty in power; his understanding has no limit.
(Psalm 147:5)

Grief is a very personal thing, and each person who experiences the loss of a spouse grieves in a unique way. Remember, only you can experience your own grief. Your grief is not an isolated incident in your life. Your entire life with your spouse is part of your personal grief. Your thoughts, feelings, emotions, and needs are yours alone. Your pain does count; don't let anyone minimize it.

Losing a spouse to death is one of the most devastating experiences you will ever face. At times it will be almost unbearable. Others have described it as deep, down-to-the-bone pain; weight so heavy, you can't stand up under it; intense sadness; a struggle just to get up in the morning; shock; numbness; and feeling dazed, confused, panicky, paralyzed, surreal, preoccupied, and angry. The list could go on and on. You may want to list additional feelings of your own. In summary, grief leaves you with a bewildering bunch of emotions. Your moods may change at the drop of a hat. Life may seem incredibly empty.

Regardless of the time or circumstances of your spouse's death, there is nothing you could have done to be prepared for it.

A note about anger. Some men/women are angry with their spouses for having "deserted" them, angry about the unfairness of the death, or just angry in general and feeling the need to blame someone. Anger is a real emotion that you must deal with. Do not let anyone tell you it is okay to be angry. It can cause much unnecessary anxiety and stress in your life. Do not deny your anger or try to repress it. Admit you are angry. Anger can destroy you if you don't get it under control. Never turn your anger inward. Seek a trusted family member or friend, a pastor (or other member of the clergy), or a biblical counselor. They will help you overcome the anger in a way that is pleasing to God and healthful and helpful to you. Unchecked anger is like a time bomb ready to explode.

"In your anger do not sin": Do not let the sun go down while you are still angry, and do not give the devil a foothold.
(Ephesians 4:26-27)

Refrain from anger and turn from wrath; do not fret—it leads only to evil.
(Psalm 37:8)

You may sleep all the time, or you may have trouble sleeping, especially at night. You may cry constantly, or you may not shed a tear. Some say they dream of their loved one or heard them speak. Some do not. Some of you may not have any of these feelings. That's you, and it's okay. None of you will display your sorrow in the exactly the same way as someone else does. Regardless of how you verbally express your feelings, you are not wrong. Never try to hide your feelings, even though, at times, it may be very difficult to show them. Let others know how you feel. If you keep your feelings bottled up inside, sooner or later they will bubble up and spill out. You may just collapse, or you may take your frustration out on another person, usually the one closest to you.

Some of you may feel you have to pretend you are doing okay, because that is what others expect. Or you must be strong and nonemotional for other family members. You think you need to be the support person, the compassionate, comforting person to everyone. Yes, this is part of grief, to be there for family members, to share feelings and emotions, to recall memories, and more. But let them know that you need comforting and emotional support also. Never refuse any type of comfort that is offered; you need, and can use, that comfort. Family and friends want to help, but they may not want to intrude on your grief. They may not know what to do. Reach out to them and let them know how they can help.

Help from others is wonderful, but now is also the time to focus on God. It will help to take your mind off yourself for a little while. Make it your goal to spend time with God and to be in His Word each day. The more you learn about Jesus and His teachings, the more you will understand yourself. It is then that you will begin to desire to live by His Word.

God is the God of comfort. God's Word (the Bible) will provide the greatest comfort. No matter how deep the pain, or how wild your emotions become, you can always turn to your Bible. God's comfort and compassion are found throughout the Bible. God is on standby, just waiting to comfort you.

"As a mother comforts her child, so will I comfort you."
(Isaiah 66:13a)

Praise be to the God and Father of our Lord, Jesus Christ, the Father of compassion and the God of all comfort.
(2 Corinthians 1:3)

For the LORD comforts his people and will have compassion on his afflicted ones.
(Isaiah 49:13b)

"I, even I, am he who comforts you."
(Isaiah 51:12a)

"But God, who comforts the downcast, comforted us."
(2 Corinthians 7:6a)

God is also your refuge in the midst of your grief, when it seems that your whole life has collapsed. He isn't just a retreat, like a summer vacation at the beach. He is a permanent and eternal refuge. He will provide the strength and endurance you need to get through any situation. Even grief!

God is our refuge and strength, an ever-present help in trouble.

(Psalm 46:1)

You have probably wanted to escape the pain of grief, as well as the sorrow, the despair, and the loneliness. God has promised to stay close to the brokenhearted. He will never leave you or forsake you.

"Never will I leave you; never will I forsake you."

(Hebrews 13:5b)

Others may tell you they know how you feel because they have lost a spouse. They may even elaborate on how terrible their grief was. Know that no one can compare their level of grief with yours. Even your closest family member or a lifelong friend cannot begin to understand what you are going through. They cannot feel the personal extent of your pain or the depth of your hurt. Your pain and hurt are yours alone.

Beware of people who say, "I know just how you feel; I've been there." They want to talk about their grief, not yours. This is a thoughtless response, although they may be well meaning. It is best to avoid those who want to talk about their own grief. You need a comforter, not a talker. There may come a time when you want to talk with people who have lost a spouse. It may help you to know how these other people got through their grief. It is your decision as to who and when you desire to talk with another. Many people might have experienced some of the same struggles you are facing, and talking with them will be helpful to you. Also know that their experiences may be completely different from yours, and thus not beneficial.

Again, I remind you, no two persons grieve the same way or within the same time frame. Even if you and another person lost your respective spouses on the same day and in the same way, you will not grieve in the same way. Nor will either of you feel the same level of pain and hurt. Your grieving time will also be very different; people are on their own individual time tables. You may need more or less time than someone else.

There may be others who think you should be "over it"; they will even give you a date. Six months to a year is what they will usually tell you. Grief can't tell time. You may move on with life more quickly and easily than others, or you may take more time and find it harder. Do not feel you must rush your grieving time. Grieving is not a newspaper with a deadline.

Each married couple has a unique relationship. No two marriages are alike, so why would you expect grieving to be the same?

Each married couple has different situations/circumstances, different joyful and different sorrowful events in their lives. All these are unique to that couple. The length of marriage at the time of loss will vary. Some of you have experienced a sudden death of your loved one, others after a long illness, or anything in between. The circumstance of your spouse's death is unlike that of any one else; no two deaths are identical.

We all need friends who will remain close and who will listen. There are times we need a friend who cares deeply, and who will offer help when help is needed. One who will share the bad times, as well as the good times. A friend who offers only a superficial friendship is of little value when you are in the middle of grief.

Even close friends cannot begin to understand the emotional ordeal you are going through. But Jesus does; He loves and understands you. He is your biggest helper during your grieving time. He is always at your side. He will give you strength to conquer all you are facing. Jesus is what you need right now.

> And my God will meet all your needs according to his glorious riches in Christ Jesus.
> (Philippians 4:19)

Family and friends can be comforters and encouragers to you. However, the comfort may only be temporary. I am not saying family/friends cannot comfort you. There were many times I needed family/friends, and they helped me. However, family/friends do have their limitations and their own lives. They may not be available when you need them the most. Or they may not be able to give you all the time you desire. There is someone who is always available for you. God never has to leave to go somewhere else. He is never too busy caring for someone else. He will always be waiting for you, to comfort you with compassionate, unfailing love. Remember, God is also taking care of your saved loved one. He has wrapped His arms around your loved one, just as He wraps His arms around you. And it was God who gave you your spouse.

May your unfailing love be my comfort, according to your promise to your servant.

(Psalm 119:76)

It's time to see your role as a friend. Even during your grieving time, it is good to seek out someone who needs a true friend. And to become that friend.

Ask God to bring into your life someone who is alone or going through a very difficult time. If you know of any grieving persons, go immediately to them. If you know nothing else to offer, give your love, your comfort, and your prayers.

Praise be to the God and Father of our Lord Jesus Christ, the Father of compassion and the God of all comfort, who comforts us in all our troubles, so that we can comfort those in trouble with the comfort we ourselves have received from God.

(2 Corinthians 1:3-4)

On a personal note, it was nearly six months before I could reach out with love to comfort others who were not close to me. I wish I had reached out sooner. Once I reached out, I found that it took my mind off myself. It forced me out of my chosen hiding place where I remained lonely and unfulfilled. The Holy Spirit renewed my desire to serve and care for others. As I put aside myself, I find I am eager to take advantage of every opportunity that comes my way.

I have emphasized that grief is unique to you for a reason. Perhaps knowing that you alone own your feelings and emotions of grief, and that others can't understand or imagine what you are going through, this may help you to realize why you may feel people have let you down, have not been there for you, have not met your needs, or do not care. When you feel alone and unsupported, turn to God and find your comfort in his Word.

Blessed are those who mourn, for they will be comforted.
(Matthew 5:4)

Precious in the sight of the LORD is the death of his saints.
(Psalm 116:15)

Needing and desiring help from another is only part of the grieving process. It is important you understand that you have a very significant, active role in your grieving. Your response to emotions, feelings, and thoughts, which are ever present, are an important part of your recovery.

I have purposefully stressed that there are no time frames for your grief. As you read the next paragraph, think about where you are in your grief. If your spouse has died recently, you may not be ready to deal with emotions, thoughts, actions, or behaviors. It's okay to wait for a short period of time. But as time goes on, and you find you are still where you were when your spouse died, you need to begin to examine your thoughts and behaviors.

You will always hang on to the good memories of your life with your spouse. They will always be a part of you. But be aware that your life will definitely change.

Only you know when you are stuck—that is, not moving forward in your grief.

Behaviors, actions, emotions, feelings, and thoughts must be examined closely before your healing can begin. Only you know which emotions/feelings are keeping you locked in your grief, or which thoughts and behaviors need to be changed, so you can move on with your life. It isn't always easy to admit that you are the one responsible for the thoughts and actions that are preventing you from having a renewed life. A life filled with joy, peace, and contentment once more. As you identify which behaviors, thoughts, and/or actions you need to change, you can then choose how you will do it. If you need help with this, seek a close trusted friend, a biblical friend, a pastor (or other member of the clergy), a biblical counselor, or a spiritual leader. They understand; they will lead you into God's Word and explain how you can apply it to your life. Just do not allow yourself to remain sorrowful and unhappy.

Grieving is not like a well-structured exercise routine. It does not come with instructions, and there are no standards that you must achieve. However, you know yourself; you know what you need and what you desire. You may even have a sense of what you need to do. You may not know the "how" or the "when". This may all sound overwhelming. If so, as you continue to read, it will become clearer. You will learn how to help yourself as you move through your grief.

For now, remember that you do not need to comply with others' expectations or listen to their advice. Also, your emotions may continue to go up and down for some time. And they will come at the most unexpected times.

What is important is that you allow yourself to grieve in your own way and in your own time. Understand your grief. When you understand grief, you will realize you are not losing your mind. Later you will sense a lessening of you pain and hurt, although it may never be completely gone. Again, there is no predictable time frame. You will heal in your own time. In order to work through your grief, you need to accept it and then find your own personal ways to deal with it.

Don't let grief dominate your life. It takes hard work to move yourself through grief. Moving on with your life is not a betrayal of your spouse. It does not mean you did not love him or her; it does not mean that you are going to forget him or her. There will be times when memories, both happy and sad, rush back into your head. These memories may seem to overwhelm you, especially when they come at the least expected times. This is part of grieving.

You may find making a decision that you would normally make with your spouse very difficult. I did. At first, I tried to think as Bud would think. *Oh he would never want the spare bedroom to be painted aqua.* I had to remind myself several times that it was okay to do as he would have desired—or not desired. It now has to be my decision. Two and a half years later I painted the bedroom aqua. It was my choice, but it was extremely hard. I did remember things that he said needed to be done. There were many home repairs that needed to be done: the house had to be restained, new gutters needed to be put up, a new furnace needed to be installed, and so on. I know it would please him to know I did those things. Each time I plant a new garden, I remember what he taught me about leveling ground, planting, and changing the oil in his tractor. These are pleasant memories. Remember, you too can recall your favorite memories anytime.

Decisions you never expected you would have to make will have to be made by you. If you choose, you may ask for help. If you do ask, that does not mean you must do as the person advised. It's still your decision to make.

Unless it is a decision that must be made immediately, give yourself some time before making that decision. You may not be thinking as clearly as you need to.

Another hurdle you will face: what to do with your spouse's things. Because each person grieves differently, there is no single answer as to when or how to do this difficult task. Some think holding on to personal items will just be reminders that their spouse is gone. Others keep the personal items around as a pleasant memory. Whichever way you choose, it is okay. But be aware there will be a time when you must do it. You may want a family member or friend to help you, or you may decide you want to do it alone. You may do it all at once, or you may do it in several different stages. Just as grieving takes time, so does making that decision. It is your decision to make; so decide what to do and then just do it. It took me two and a half years before I could even think about it. Most of Bud's personal things have been given away or taken to Goodwill. I do have a couple of totes with things I've wanted to keep for the kids, grandkids, or others. And of course, some things I want to keep for me. I still wear his quilted flannel shirts and his boots (for shoveling snow). His Navy uniform still hangs in the closet.

So mourn and grieve as you desire, but also make the best of your present life. Live as God intended. He desires that your life be filled with love, joy, peace, and all the good things He provides. Let God lead and guide you. He is the Great Physician, and He will help you overcome your grief.

Maybe you have always been the strong one, not showing weakness. True strength doesn't mean you can't show emotions. May be you are very independent. Recognize you have limitations. Admit when you are weak, tired, and even exhausted. When you are confused, anxious, and/or stressed let family and friends help you. Remember, you are in control of you; you can decide when, where, and how you need the help. After you have found a person to help, accept that help. Sometimes you may not realize you need help; if someone suggests some help, accept it graciously. It is often difficult to have someone come into your house to help you. But when you do it, is a blessing to you and to the other person.

God has put those special people in your life. He did not intend for you to suffer alone. I learned the hard way—trying to be strong and independent is a very lonely way to grieve.

It may be very difficult, when you are the one struggling, to be mindful of others and their feelings. However, if you were to initiate a conversation about your spouse, it may be the opportunity they have been waiting for. They may not be aware that you desire to share thoughts of your spouse. If the person or people you are talking to are not responsive, it may be that they are not ready to talk about your spouse; they may also be grieving the loss of your spouse. Seek out someone else.

Remember to give yourself permission to grieve, and don't put a date when you will be over it. Let your feelings be seen by others. This is a positive action for you. Don't try to be superman/woman.

Go ahead and cry when you need to. Do not hold back those tears; just let them fall, anytime and anywhere. If others are uncomfortable, that's their problem, not yours. You are taking care of your emotional well-being. It is not your job to make everyone feel at ease and comfortable. It may help to find someone who is close to you, someone who will cry with you. Remember, Jesus wept when He was sad.

Jesus wept.
(John 11:35)

Throughout your grief, the hardest emotion to overcome is probably loneliness. It is an overpowering, overwhelming feeling to be alone in a familiar setting: your home. There is a surreal, disorientating component, as if all normal surroundings were smashed and hidden under an engulfing layer of darkness.

You may just sit and stare, trying to compose yourself. Trying to focus on what is real, what has happened, why it happened, and what to do now. Answers are difficult to find at this time. Your mind feels like it has been anesthetized, yet the anesthetic has not numbed the pain.

At this time, your thoughts are your enemy. They will keep you locked in the misery of loneliness.

Being without a spouse means you will be by yourself much of the time. But you are never alone. God is always near you, and He promises never to leave you. You are not alone in your pain and suffering; nor are you alone in your grief.

[F]or the LORD, your God goes with you; he will never leave you nor forsake you.

Deuteronomy 31:6b

You can talk to God any time. He will always hear you and will always listen. Tell Him of your pain, your loneliness; ask Him to strengthen and encourage you, to heal your broken heart.

Being lonely really is an issue of the heart. Right now your heart is broken, and it feels like it is surrounded by an impregnable darkness. God can penetrate that darkness. He is standing near you, waiting for you to reach out to Him. He wants to take away your darkness and replace it with his radiant light.

"Do not be afraid, for I am with you."

(Isaiah 43:5)

"I will turn the darkness into light before them
and make the rough places smooth.
These are the things I will do;
I will not forsake them."

(Isaiah 42:16b, c)

You are my lamp, O LORD;
the LORD turns my darkness into light.

(2 Samuel 22:29)

You, O LORD, keep my lamp burning;
my God turns my darkness into light.
(Psalm 18:28)

Though I sit in darkness, the LORD will be my light.
(Micah 7:8b)

God will take care of you; you are His beloved one. He will help you through whatever difficult situation you are facing.

Light in the Bible is a symbol of God's presence, His works, His holiness and His purity. Light represents God's truth, goodness, and redemptive work. The term is used to enlighten, to provide knowledge, and to guide. To be in God's light is to know God and desire to obey Him. His light enables us to be free from sin and Satan's deception. Let God's light shine as you take every troubling, hurting thought to God.

We demolish arguments and every pretension that sets itself up against the knowledge of God, and we take captive every thought to make it obedient to Christ.
(2 Corinthians 10:5)

You must capture every thought you have and yield it to God. When you are thinking negative, hurting, painful thoughts, you have a choice. You can continue to dwell on these unhealthy thoughts, thereby pulling yourself deeper into despair and darkness, or you can admit their destructive nature and then submit them all to God.

Ask Him to redirect your thinking. Ask Him to help you focus on Him and His Word.

This is not easy. It takes practice and discipline on your part. The benefit of being close to God and being free from those negative, harmful thoughts will bring you peace and rest. You will experience a state of calm that you haven't felt for a long time.

God will provide whatever you need.

Support:

When I said, "My foot is slipping," your love, O Lᴏʀᴅ, supported me.

(Psalm 94:18)

Encouragement and strength:

May our Lord Jesus Christ himself and God our Father, who loved us and by his grace gave us eternal encouragement and good hope, encourage your hearts and strengthen you in every good deed and word.

(2 Thessalonians 2:16-17)

Love:

For God so loved the world that he gave his only begotten Son, that whosoever believeth in him should not perish, but have everlasting life.

(John 3:16 [KJV])

Although it is difficult to imagine it now, there will come a time when you will be able to laugh again. Both Jesus and Solomon talked about laughing after mourning.

Blessed are you who weep now, for you will laugh.

(Luke 6:21b)

[A] time to weep and a time to laugh a time to mourn and a time to dance.

(Ecclesiastes 3:4)

Solomon reminds you that there is a time to cry and a time to laugh. Both laughing and crying are under your control. Do look for the funny things that happen and take the time to laugh. It really is good medicine.

A cheerful heart is good medicine but a crushed spirit dries up the bones.

(Proverbs 17:22)

Think about little children. How spontaneous and joyful is their laughter. It makes you laugh just to hear them.

Laughter between two adults can make a difficult day much better. When you're feeling down and alone you need a friend who will bring out a happy little chuckle or a great big belly laugh. Friends are able to prompt a memory of a funny event or a special person.

Laughter is a stress reliever. When your emotions are out of control, stress has beaten you into the ground, and you are ready to explode, just laugh. Even if you are alone, find something to laugh about.

Or call that special witty friend who always makes you laugh over the silliest things. The call will spark laughter and perhaps a few tears. What a way to get out all those bottled-up emotions that you're hidden within your heart.

Maybe the friend you called needed a laugh even more than you did. A double blessing.

On a personal note, my cousin Katie and I call each other often. We laugh over the craziest things. We talk for over an hour, even when we don't have anything to say. Once when Bud and I were leaving Katie and Bill's house, Bill said, "Connie, hurry home so Katie can call you."

And she did.

When your day appears cloudy and gray, put on a smile, and the sun will shine. Even if you are alone, smile. If you are old enough, you will remember an old song that went something like this:

"Put on your old gray bonnet with the blue ribbons on it
And smile, smile, smile."

That's good advice. Any time you are with others, put on a happy smile. A genuine smile is a sign of affirmation or of appreciation and love. Your smile can bring hope and positive change into a person's life today.

Give a smile away today. Count how many you get in return.

This reminds me of an incident several years ago. I was going through a very difficult time. I was grocery shopping. Two ladies passed me, and they each smiled. *Don't smile at me,* I thought, *I have nothing to smile about.* As they walked past, I heard one of them say, "She could have at least smiled back."

That memory has stayed with me. Now I realize that if I had smiled back, it might have made me feel better, even if only while in the store. It certainly would have made those ladies happy. Since that time, I have tried to smile to others as I shop.

There is another side to that incident. A warning: be careful. If you smile at people who don't smile back, give them some grace. You don't know what problems/difficulties they may be facing. They could be hurting physically, emotionally, or spiritually. They may be out of work or perhaps just experienced the loss of a loved one. A heavy burden might weigh them down, or their minds may be elsewhere. Don't be annoyed or judge too quickly. Even if they do not smile back, your smile may have cheered them up a little. Say a little prayer for them.

Perhaps, right now, you are feeling a little overwhelmed with all you have read. You may be thinking this is just too much to comprehend or to put into practice. You are having trouble concentrating and remembering everything. Don't worry; that is normal and it is also part of grieving.

To help you, I am offering a few of God's promises. I suggest you read them daily; they will lift you up, encourage you, and provide you with strength, comfort, and peace. God and I both desire to ease your hurting, sad troubled heart and mind.

Only within God's Word will you find all the answers you need to restore, reawaken, revive, and motivate you into applying His Word to your life now. He will give you unbelievable strength and power to live the abundant life He desires for you.

Here are some quick references to some of God's promises. Keep these near you. You will also find many more in your Bible.

God is always near you, and He promises never to leave you. You are not alone in your pain and suffering:

[F]or the LORD your God goes with you; he will never leave you nor forsake you.

(Deuteronomy 31:6b)

God's grace is sufficient:

But he said to me, "My grace is sufficient for you."
(2 Corinthians 12:9a)

May our Lord Jesus Christ himself and God our Father, who
loved us and by his grace gave us eternal encouragement and
good hope . . .
(2 Thessalonians 2:16)

He will supply all your needs:

And my God will meet all your needs according to his
glorious riches in Christ Jesus.
(Philippians 4:19)

God's love is unfailing and endures forever:

May your unfailing love rest upon us, O Lord, even as we
put our hope in you.
(Psalm 33:22)

May your unfailing love be my comfort, according to your
promise to your servant.
(Psalm 119:76)

Give thanks to the Lord, for he is good; his love endures
forever.
(1 Chronicles 16:34)

God's watch care is continuous; He never sleeps:

From his dwelling place he watches all who live on earth.
(Psalm 33:14)

He will not let your foot slip—
he who watches over you will not slumber;
The Lord will keep you from all harm—
he will watch over your life;

the LORD will watch over your coming and your going
both now and forevermore.

(Psalm 121:3, 7-8)

God promises to help you:

I lift up my eyes to the hills—
where does my help come from?
My help comes from the LORD,
the Maker of heaven and earth.

(Psalm 121:1-2)

God is merciful:

The LORD our God is merciful and forgiving, even though
we have rebelled against him.

(Daniel 9:9)

Grace, mercy and peace from God the Father and Christ
Jesus our Lord.

(1 Timothy 1:2b)

The Lord is full of compassion and mercy.

(James 5:11b)

God will fill your life with peace. Only in Christ Jesus will you find
true peace:

And the peace of God, which transcends all understanding,
will guard your hearts and your minds in Christ Jesus.

(Philippians 4:7)

Jesus will carry your burdens. But you must be willing to give them to
Him:

Praise be to the LORD, to God our Savior,
who daily bears our burdens. Selah

(Psalm 68:19)

Jesus will give you rest when you are weary:

"Come to me, all you who are weary and burdened, and I will give you rest."

(Matthew 11:28)

Maybe you are wondering, *How do I talk to God? How do I ask for peace, rest, comfort, and mercy? How do I ask Him to carry my burdens?* God always has an answer and a way. God talks to us through his Word, and we talk to God through our prayers.

Prayer is communication with God. God is a loving, caring Father who desires a personal relationship with his children. God encourages us in His Word to come to Him in prayer.

Everyone can offer prayers to God. However, the effectiveness of prayer depends upon a spiritually informed response of each individual who is saved by grace. Our prayers reach heaven and are heard by God because the barrier between God and people was removed when Christ paid the penalty on the cross for our sins. He died, was buried, and rose again, so that all humanity would be freed from the power of sin and have eternal life in God's kingdom. (For additional information regarding salvation, please see part VII of this book, "Plan of Salvation.")

God does hear every prayer, and He answers each one in His way and in His time.

There is much to learn about prayer from God's Word.

Jesus also prayed:

Very early in the morning, while it was still dark, Jesus got up, left the house and went off to a solitary place, where he prayed.

(Mark 1:35)

Prayers:

The widow who is really in need and left alone puts her hope in God and continues night and day to pray and ask for help.

(1 Timothy 5:5)

(Note: the previous scripture also applies to widowers.)

Answer me when I call to you,
O my righteous God.
Give me relief from my distress;
be merciful to me and hear my prayer.
(Psalm 4:1)

The LORD heard my cry for mercy;
the LORD accepts my prayer.
(Psalm 6:9)

On reaching the place, he said to them, "Pray that you do not fall into temptation."
(Luke 22:40)

Be joyful always; pray continually; give thanks in all circumstances, for this is God's will for you in Christ Jesus.
(1 Thessalonians 5:16-18)

God hears your prayers:

For the eyes of the Lord are on the righteous and his ears are attentive to their prayers.
(1 Peter 3:12a)

[A]nd God heard them, for their prayer reached heaven, his holy dwelling place.
(2 Chronicles 30:27b)

God answers prayers:

So we fasted and petitioned our God about this, and he answered our prayer.
(Ezra 8:23)

He answered their payers, because they trusted him.
(1 Chronicles 5:20b)

A familiar prayer, the Lord's Prayer:

And it came to pass, that, as he was praying in a certain place, when he ceased, one of his disciples said unto him, "Lord, teach us to pray, as John also taught his disciples."

And he said unto them, "When ye pray, say, Our Father which art in heaven,

Hallowed be thy name. Thy kingdom come. Thy will be done, as in heaven, so in earth

Give us day by day our daily bread.

And forgive us our sins; for we also forgive every one that is indebted to us.

And lead us not into temptation; but deliver us from evil."

(Luke 11:1-4 [New King James Study Bible])

A final note: grieving takes time, and it requires help from God. It doesn't happen the way you wish it would. You will never forget the pain and sorrow. Nor will you ever forget your spouse and your life together. However, life does have a way of moving on. Some family and friends will remain close; others may not. New friends will come into your life. New things will happen. God doesn't leave you stalled forever. He knows when it is time for you to move on. With gentle nudges, He will lead you into new and better things. It is a new beginning in life. God urges you to look for new meaning in life by looking to Him. Your purpose in life is found in God's Word. It is always available, reliable, and true. God will fill you with all you need to give your life some meaning and joy once more.

"For I know the plans I have for you," declares the LORD, "plans to prosper you and not to harm you, plans to give you hope and a future."

(Jeremiah 29:11)

Personal Actions for a Grieving Person

$\mathcal{F}$irst, acknowledge that grieving will take hard work, determination, and time. Acknowledge that you are the only one responsible for your grief. You will need to allow yourself time to grieve. Trying to ignore or holding in your feelings/emotions, and/or pretending, can only make matters worse and will prolong your grieving time. Letting out painful emotions and thoughts will help you heal.

Second, keep in mind that personal habits and daily routines, including eating and sleeping, will probably change; interests may also change, as well as priorities. You do not have to explain these changes to others. If you choose to share, be honest.

Third, it is important that you assume the responsibility for overcoming your grief and establishing your recovery.

Take Care of Yourself

Grief can, and will, take a heavy toll on your physical, emotional, and mental state. Physically you need to get enough rest and sleep. You may even need to take naps. An adequate diet is essential. You may have a decreased appetite or a loss of appetite; or you may experience uncontrollable eating. You may have little or no desire to cook. You may gain or lose weight. Try to maintain your normal weight. Sleep and diet are among the most important physical aspects in overcoming grief. You must keep up your strength. You may have to actually set times to eat; try eating small nutritious meals and snacks frequently throughout the day. Choose healthy food. It may be helpful to set regular times to go to bed and to get up. If you neglect your physical needs, you may become weak, overly tired, and even ill. If your physical needs are not met, all aspects of grieving will be stalled.

Exercise Is Beneficial

Regular exercise improves both body and mind. Exercising will refresh you and help to take your mind off yourself, your pain, and your hurt. Even if you only walk a short distance a day, you will feel better. You may have a preferred exercise routine that you have done in the past. Now is the time to resume that routine. Walking, jogging, biking, exercising with videos, and weight lifting are only a few of the possibilities. Later you may choose to join a gym or find a new type of exercise.

Science has shown that exercise releases a chemical substance in the brain that makes you feel better.

Please consult your health care provider before starting any exercise program or weight-loss regimen/diet.

Look to Your Faith

If you have allowed grief to shatter your faith, or if you just want to get close to God once more, there are many ways to return to God. Confess and repent of your sins. We have a loving and faithful Father. He will welcome you back with open arms. For inspiration, look to nature or a Bible-teaching church. Attend a Bible study, read and study God's Word daily, learn his truths and promises. Rejoice in our Lord and Savior and the eternal salvation He offers freely. Find comfort in:

Attending church
Praying and meditating
Fellowships at your place of worship
Being with other believers
Serving your church and others
Reading spiritual resources and your Bible

Dealing with Past Regrets

Don't beat yourself up over past regrets, those that continue to be in your thoughts. The "if only"s and the "should have"s. Just take a step back, take a deep breath, and stop your thoughts. Accept the fact that you were doing the best you could at that time. Everyone makes mistakes. But there are no "do overs" in life. Now is the time to leave the regrets of the past in the past. They will only keep you from moving on into your new life.

Keeping a Journal

This is an opportunity to write anything you choose. No one will ever read it except you. You can be honest about good or bad feelings, emotions, thoughts, and behaviors. It is also a time to talk with God through your writing. Use this time to thank Him for your blessings, and also to ask Him to take away your sadness and to heal your broken heart. You can say anything that is on your mind to God. (He already knows your thoughts.) You can even ask Him questions. You can also jot down Scriptures in your journal.

Also include things you want to accomplish, as well as things you have accomplished. Things you may be thinking/wondering about. You can write about anything at all; there are no limitations, restrictions, or instructions.

You may enjoy creative writing, and this is an excellent place to keep it.

Journaling is really a healing tool. You can see where you have been, where you are now, and everything in between. During those days when the pain returns and is unbearable, writing about it will help. Writing will also keep you connected to God. Give it a try. You don't have to be a great writer; just be sincere and honest with yourself. Remember, only you will read your journal.

Keep a Schedule

A schedule is helpful. It will help restore stability to your life. However, do not make it too rigid; leave room for unexpected things and some time to be spontaneous. Be sure to schedule some time for enjoyment each day. At first, this may be something you enjoy doing at home. As your energy returns, venture outside your house for an afternoon or evening. Call a friend and make plans to get together. Isolation is an enemy.

Resume Your Friendships as soon as Possible

This may be difficult at first. You may have to make the first call to set a date. Family and friends may be hesitant to call, fearing you are not ready for company. Remember, they do not know where you are in your grief. Invite them over for coffee or tea. You can also suggest doing the things you used to do with them.

You may find it difficult to be with couples, especially if the four of you did things together. You may feel that it's a couples' society and you no longer fit in. You may want to stay at home because you do not have a partner to do things with. You can invite couples to your home. Tell them you miss them and would like to see them again. Some couples will respond favorably, and others will not. They may be grieving the loss of your spouse also. Give them time to accept that your spouse is gone. Do not be afraid to ask them about their grief. As time goes by, you may want to contact them again, or they may contact you, and your friendship will resume.

Even personal friends and family may begin to act differently. They may be struggling with the death of your spouse also. They need time to heal, as they have suffered a loss also. Give them some time and then try to reconnect once again.

As time passes, it may be necessary to reevaluate some of your friendships. You may even need to move on and find new friends. Wait awhile before you make that decision; everyone needs time to heal.

Reach Out to Others

Now is the time to reach out to others. Don't make your home a hiding place. This may seem overwhelming to you. You may still be trying to just maintain yourself, struggling to get through one day at a time. However, when you reach out to help others, you will begin to look beyond yourself and your grief. There are many people who need love, comfort, and a caring friend.

Now is the time to serve God. If you have been serving, continue. If you have not served, now is the time to start. Find places in your church and community; volunteer at shelters for the poor, in schools, local nursing homes, children's reading groups, or at the library. Be a guide at a local museum. There are many ways to volunteer your time and be of service. If handy with tools, do repairs for others. If you sing or play an instrument, use that talent to bring joy to others. Use your skills and abilities to teach a child. Write a book. The list of what you can do to help, support, encourage, and show love to others truly is limitless.

Counseling and Support Groups

Support groups conducted by a trained biblical counselor or sponsored by a church can help you learn how to deal with your feelings, emotions, and thoughts. They also teach Scriptures that relate to your grief and healing. Support groups are helpful for many, as they are structured with definite guidelines. However, as it is a group setting, you may not receive the individual attention you desire.

You may prefer counseling from a biblical counselor, a pastor, or a clergy member. You may find it easier to talk with someone you do not know personally. A biblical counselor is trained and certified. They have techniques that will show you how to overcome your grief by trusting in God's Word and His promises. They can help you to understand your grief and the need to turn to God for your healing. They will help you find the spiritual resources you need.

I encourage you to research each person or program before starting. Be sure that they will meet your needs. They should show you how to reach out to God, who gives His power and strength to overcome every situation/circumstance that comes in your life.

Some words of warning: If your grief becomes so severe that you feel you cannot continue with your daily routine, *you must seek professional help*. If you stop taking care of yourself and your house, you refuse to leave your house, you stop answering your phone, you aren't eating enough, you aren't bathing properly, you refuse to see anyone, you experience extreme fatigue day after day, you stop taking prescribed medications, you stay in bed most of the time, you sleep all the time or do not sleep at all, or if you exhibit any other unusual symptoms, you must seek professional help.

Do not delay! Grief that is so debilitating that it interferes with all your daily living activities, needs to be dealt with now by a trained professional. You will not be able to overcome it yourself.

Avoid alcohol and nonprescription drugs. Trying to escape your pain by using alcohol or pain medication will only delay your grief. They will ultimately create new problems. If your health-care provider prescribes medication, ask about the risks and side effects. Types of medication that are frequently overprescribed and misused are anti-anxiety drugs, sleeping pills, and pain relievers. If your health-care provider prescribes any of these, take them with caution and for a short time only. Continued and frequent follow-up is necessary.

Things to Do on Your Own

You will have to stretch yourself and do new things. You will probably be uncomfortable as you begin to do things by yourself and on your own. There are many things that can be done without a partner.

1. *Go to a bookstore.* Some stores allow you to take magazines and books to their cafés, where you can sit and read.
2. *Go shopping.* Not just for groceries. You can get some exercise by walking through the mall. You do not need to buy anything.
3. *Go out to eat.* This may be difficult for many of you. Remember, single people eat out alone all the time. A safe first place is the food court at your local mall. These areas are usually busy with people coming and going. Many are eating alone. Once you are comfortable at the food court, move on to a restaurant.
4. *Take a class.* Continuing-education classes are offered for personal development or college credit. If you haven't kept up with technology, there are many beginner classes that teach how to use a computer. And if you have kept up with technology, there are many varied classes offered online.
5. *Take a vacation.* An easy way to take a first-time solo vacation is to go with a tour group. You can choose a cruise, a historic tour, or a bus tour (in the US or another country). There are so many travel opportunities. Of course, if you prefer to travel with someone, invite a family member or a friend to join you.
6. *Pursue a hobby.* Continue with hobbies you enjoy or start a new one. Invest your time in learning something new—sewing, quilting, cooking, woodworking, remodeling projects, gardening, etc. You

know what you like to do—and what you've always wanted to do but never had time.

7. *Entertain.* If you have enjoyed entertaining in the past, continue. You may need to entertain on a smaller scale until your energy has returned. Don't try to do too much, too soon.

8. *Get a new pet.* Some people find caring for and loving a pet relieves stress and brings them joy. This is not for everyone.

Suggested Activities

Read a new book or read to others.

Write personal letters or letters for others.

Take a walk.

Knit or crochet for various charities (lap blankets, prayer shawls, etc.).

Have a tea party with your best friend or a little child.

Watch a DVD.

Go to a movie or take someone to a movie.

Visit a nursing home.

Call a friend.

Call a relative.

Clean an elderly person's home.

Play piano or other instruments.

Get a group together to sing.

Go Christmas caroling.

Visit people who can't get out.

Become the photographer for friends and family.

Write your life story.

Surprise someone by taking supper to him or her.

Give lots of love and hugs to those who need a friend.

Laugh, laugh, and laugh.

Sit with a friend and ask to hear his or her life story; listen attentively.

Volunteer at a local hospital, nursing home, or homeless shelter—extend love to all.

Make crafts for the holidays and give them away to people you don't know (or to friends and family).

Take up a new hobby: scrapbooking, cooking, gardening, woodworking, repair work, etc.

Do home repairs for someone in need.

Get a pet.
Be a comforter and encourager to someone.
Reach out to people.
Pick wildflowers and bring a bouquet to someone.
Be creative. You know your interest and hobbies.
You know people who need help; help them.
Serve in your local church; if you don't have a church, find one and
attend services regularly.
Ask other people for suggestions.
Go on a picnic.
Learn to play golf or take someone golfing.
Go fishing or take someone fishing.
Take a child to the circus, to play miniature golf, or to eat at
McDonald's.
Learn a new sport.

Helping a Grieving Person

When people are in the deepest depths of grief, there may be nothing you can do except be with them. Grievers need to know you still want to be part of their lives. At this time, they feel isolated and apart from everyone. Don't put off or avoid seeing them for the first time. Think about their being alone, not about your own discomfort. Don't make excuses to yourself as to why you can't go. When you visit for the first time, if you are not really close to them, do not stay too long. If you are close, you will sense when it is time to leave. As you leave, ask when would be a good time to visit again. Make a date to do so. Never say you will visit and then not visit, unless you have an emergency.

As you sit down to talk, be relaxed. Clear your mind of all distractions. Now is the time to sit quietly, letting the grievers talk and share as desired. When you are quiet, it allows others to talk. Silence makes most people very uncomfortable; however, silence can be very beneficial when helping others. Learn to listen; really listen, don't just stop talking, but listen. You may realize you don't have to speak at all. Silently sitting with people shows that you care about them. Being a good listener is very important. Most people are better talkers than listeners. Now is the time to practice the art of listening. It takes discipline on your part to be a top-notch listener. It isn't always easy to stay quiet and let others talk.

My dear brothers, take note of this: everyone should be quick to listen, slow to speak and slow to become angry.
(James 1:19)

Do not interrupt with your own feelings, emotions, thoughts, or advice. When you are quiet, those grieving feel valued and know that you want to hear what they have to say.

Let the grievers lead the conversation. If they remain quiet, you are to also remain quiet. However, if the silence continues for a very long time, you may decide to speak. Evaluate the length of time very carefully. Grievers may have trouble knowing where to start; allow ample time for them to feel composed and ready to speak. Grieving persons often try to cover up their feelings and thoughts. At this time, they may not know or be able to say what they need or how they are really feeling. Remember, all their thoughts are on their loved one being gone.

Be sensitive to their needs. Set aside your own needs and desires; concentrate totally on those you came to help. Grievers may be hesitant to share personal thoughts. After listening, it may be necessary to ask some basic questions. You may need to prompt the conversation. It is better to ask questions that cannot be answered by a simple yes or no. If you ask a question, such as: "Are you doing okay?" or "Are you sad today?" Those asked will answer with a yes or no. It is better to say, "You seem to be deep in thought right now. I care about you and want to be here for you. What can I do right now to help?" or "I can see you are really hurting. Let me share that hurt with you. I will be here when you are ready to talk about your hurt or anything that's on your mind."

Occasionally, it helps to repeat what was said, for clarification. This should not be done often and should always be done very discreetly. You may say, "I heard you say you are very sad and you don't know what to do. Let's talk about this a little more." If you use this technique too often, you will begin to sound like a parrot, which can be very irritating to others.

Many persons, although well meaning, have failed in their attempts to comfort or help those grieving. Often they did not know what to say or what to do. So they said and did what they had heard or seen others do. Thus, they give worldly advice that matches worldly values. Below are some worldly sayings and beliefs people have. **Be careful not to repeat these to any grieving persons.** Personally I do not think any of these are true:

Anyone who has faith, does not need to grieve.
Strong people are able to get through grief on their own. They don't need help from others.

A strong person doesn't show emotions. Do not cry in front of people.

If you cry, you are weak.

You will be okay in about six months.

Don't let your feelings be seen by others.

Older people handle grief more easily than young people. They have had more experience.

Don't ask God questions or be angry at God; it means your faith is weak.

People who grieve longer prove they loved their spouses more than someone who gets over grief quickly.

When your grief is over, you can move on with your life, and you won't think about your spouse.

Christians shouldn't grieve if they know their loved one is in heaven.

Give grieving people self-help books on grieving so they don't rely on their emotions

Don't allow grieving people to talk about their spouses; it will just prolong their grief.

To grieve properly, you go through certain stages. When completed, your grief will be over. However, you must go through each stage before going on to the next.

After your spouse dies, you will never be truly happy again.

Don't make any financial decisions for at least six months.

If you don't put flowers on your spouse's grave or visit the grave often, you didn't love him or her very much.

Do not get married again for at least a year.

You may have heard other sayings that you could add to the ones listed above.

Acknowledge that you do not have all the answers, but you do care about those grieving and have time to spend with them. It doesn't matter if you have or have not lost a spouse; be honest and tell them you cannot possibly understand the depth of their grief. If you have lost a spouse, do not compare your grief with theirs. Do not say, "I know how you feel." Because you do not! Grief is unique to each person.

Others may relate losing a spouse to losing a family member or close friend. This should not be done. It's like comparing apples to oranges. The relationship between a husband and wife is a unique relationship established by God. There is no other relationship like it. Just as each relationship we have is unique.

This is also true of a divorce. The divorced person feels a loss unlike any other loss, regardless of the circumstances. Do not make a mistake and compare your divorce with losing a spouse. This occurred with me, and I felt that my emotions and feelings had been minimized and were not important.

Katie, my very caring cousin said to me, "I can't imagine how you feel," I replied "no you cannot. Just imagine getting up every morning and not having Bill to have coffee with. And knowing you never will see him again on this earth."

If those grieving decide to confide in you, remain silent. Just let them talk. They need an understanding family member or friend. Do not give advice early on in their grief process. If you are close to them, they may ask for advice. You will know when it's time and what advice to give. Leading them to Scripture is the best advice you can give. They will then do God's will in God's way.

Many people have the habit of thinking about other things while another person is talking to them. Clear your mind of distractions. Look at those speaking. Let them know that you are hearing and concentrating on everything said. If your thoughts are loving and kind, your words will be also.

Carry each other's burdens, and in this way you will fulfill
the law of Christ.

(Galatians 6:2)

Do not judge what those grieving have to say. For example, don't say things like, "You shouldn't feel that way" or "there is no need to feel so sad." Acknowledge his or her feelings by saying something like, "You're very sad right now, aren't you?"

Help those grieving remember the good times, and if they choose, some sad times. As time goes on, encourage them to think and talk less about the sad times and focus on the present and the future. Let them share their precious memories with you. Encourage them to share whatever they choose. You can also share your memories of their spouses. It is really uplifting and joyful, to those grieving, to have someone share memories of and experiences with their lost spouses. To know that their spouses were special to another person is extremely precious to those grieving. However, do not monopolize the conversation with your own memories/experiences. The time spent recalling memories is also a time of making new memories. Those grieving will remember your thoughtfulness, your wanting to spend time with them. And later will recall with special remembrance that you wanted to share their grief and pain and were available and willing to help when most needed.

This is one of the most important roles you can play: that of a comforter. Letting those grieving know that you are, and will always be, available when they need you. However, at this time, they may not know what those needs are, or they may be unable to verbalize them. Your presence is a comfort, and it provides security to those who are now alone.

As a comforter, you give hope, encouragement, reassurance, strength, and help to a lonely, often confused, weary, sad person. Your speech and attitude should be pleasant, sincere, genuine, and nurturing. Those grieving should feel special and cared for, as if wrapped tightly in strong, loving arms.

His left arm is under my head and his right arm embraces me.
(Song of Songs 1:3)

Spend some time reading Scripture to those grieving. God is the Great Comforter. They will find the comfort they need in God's Word. Help him or her to understand and apply God's Word of comfort to his or her life today.

Blessed are those who mourn for they will be comforted.
(Matthew 5:4)

May your unfailing love be my comfort, according to your promise to your servant.
(Psalm 119:76)

"Then maidens will dance and be glad,
young men and old as well.
I will turn their mourning into gladness;

GRIEVING FOR THE GLORY OF GOD

I will give them comfort and joy instead of sorrow."
(Jeremiah 31:13)

Everyone has the ability to help others who are hurting emotionally and spiritually. There are no exact guidelines to follow. One of the most important ways of helping those grieving is to shower them with sincere, unconditional love. We love people because they have been made in God's image. We are all God's creation.

So God created man in his own image, in the image of God he created him; male and female he created them.
(Genesis 1:27)

What is love? How do we show love to others?

Sometimes love becomes a word with very mixed messages. In the world today, love is a word used frequently and with little meaning. Some people say, "I love you," as easily as they say, "good morning." People sign letters, "with love," to mere acquaintances. On television we often hear some preachers yelling out, "Just feel the love in this room," as the camera catches many bored and uninvolved faces. Those of us who remember the 1960s and '70s will recall how love could change the world.

The Webster's Seventh New Collegiate Dictionary defines love as, "to hold dear; to cherish; devotion or tenderness; to take pleasure in; to feel affection or experience desire."

God's Word tells us that love is an attribute of God and an essential part of His holy nature.

Whoever does not love does not know God, because God is love.
(1 John 4:8)

God calls us to show genuine love. Genuine love that goes beyond just being polite. God speaks of true love as being unselfish; it involves caring and loving others, even if it means sacrificing oneself. There are many verses that speak of God's love and His commandments regarding love:

For God so loved the world that he gave his only begotten Son, that whosoever believeth in him should not perish, but have everlasting life.

(John 3:16 [NKJ])

A new commandment I give you: Love one another. As I have loved you, so you must love one another.

(John 13:34)

And now these three remain: faith, hope and love. But the greatest is love.

(1 Corinthians 13:13)

Do everything in love.

(1 Corinthians 16:14)

We love because he first loved us.

(1 John 4:19)

And so we know and rely on the love God has for us. God is love. Whoever lives in love lives in God, and God in him.

(1 John 4:16)

Be completely humble and gentle; be patient, bearing with one another in love.

(Ephesians 4:2)

Be devoted to one another in brotherly love. Honor one another above yourselves.

(Romans 12:10)

Hurting, grieving people need an abundance of love. True love instinctively lets you know what is needed. You need to set aside your own feelings and thinking. Just sit quietly and concentrate on the ones grieving. Look at their faces and posture, and then listen carefully to what they say. Nonverbal clues will also help. Such verbal and nonverbal clues as crying or not crying, nervousness, anxiety, rambling speech or complete silence, expressions or lack of expressions, are a few to watch for. Knowing the grievers will also help you to identify these clues.

No one has ever been able to package or bottle the absolute and perfect response to another's personal suffering. Some who are grieving may want someone to distract their thoughts and pain, if only for a little while, with cheerfulness and enthusiasm. Others find this approach distasteful. Some want honest, straight talk; others find this to be depressing and discouraging. You have to get to know these people as grievers, not merely as the friends or family members you used to know. Perhaps you do not know each grieving person personally. Friends or acquaintances, you must get to know them. The only way to do that is to spend quality time listening. There is no instant magical cure for people who are hurting and mourning the loss of a spouse.

There are many simple ways to show compassion and love. You may be a person who likes to hug. Remember, not everyone is comfortable with physical touching. But to those who are, a big strong hug in the midst of hurting circumstances speaks volumes. A little smile is always appropriate. Greeting those grieving with a warm, genuine smile tells them, "I'm so glad to see you." The unspoken message is "I want to be here with you."

The love of a caring family member/friend is priceless. Remember, your friend or loved one is wounded, broken by the death of a spouse. Those grieving seek a loving person committed to staying for as long as it takes. They need a friend to fill their broken hearts with hope. They long for you to be part of their lives and to help them find hope for the future. Even if you do not know these people very well, you can always give hope, comfort, and love. This could be the start of new and lasting friendships.

Be strong and take heart, all you who hope in the LORD.
(Psalm 31:24)

Find rest, O my soul, in God alone; my hope comes from him.
(Psalm 62:5)

Be joyful in hope, patient in affliction, faithful in prayer.
(Romans 12:12)

May the God of hope fill you with all joy and peace as you trust in him, so that you may overflow with hope by the power of the Holy Spirit.

(Romans 15:13)

As you love, care for, and bring hope to those grieving, encourage them to seek God. He knows their pain and suffering. He knows they are weary. He wants to give them rest.

Come to me, all you who are weary and burdened, and I will give you rest.

(Matthew 11:28)

They can also lay all their burdens at God's feet:

Praise be to the LORD, to God our Savior, who daily bears our burdens. Selah

(Psalm 68:19)

You must also be willing to carry burdens for others:

Carry each other's burdens, and in this way you will fulfill the law of Christ.

(Galatians 6:2)

Another way to show love is through prayer. Praying with, and for, the grieving person is one of the greatest gifts you can give. Prayer is very powerful medicine. God is waiting to hear your prayers for the special people you are helping. As you sit with those grieving, put your arm around them, or hold hands and tell them Jesus loves them; tell them you love them and are praying for them. Ask them how you can pray for them. And pray each day, even if you are not with them.

[P]ray for each other, so that you may be healed. The prayer of a righteous person is powerful and effective.

(James 5:16b)

With this in mind, we constantly pray for you.
(2 Thessalonians 1:11a)

[As you help us by your prayers. Then many will give thanks on our behalf for the gracious favor granted us in answer to the prayers of many.
(2 Corinthians 1:11)

God hears every prayer, and He answers each one in His way and in His time.

When you are with those grieving, keep in mind that, at the peak of pain, they do not need your knowledge or advice. What they need is just to be able to rest in your comfort and your love, having the assurance that you will be there whenever needed.

If you think you are inadequate to be that special person to those grieving, think again. God uses ordinary people to help bring about His healing. He can, and will, use you. Ask God how He wants to use you. He will lead you in unimaginable ways. Just ask yourself, "Am I willing to be that friend? To always be available? To know I must sacrifice my time and energy whenever needed?"

You may only be one person, but you may be the only one to the griever(s).

When you are sitting with the griever(s) and you truly want to show your love, think before you say anything. Ask yourself, "Is what I am about to say encouraging, supportive, and comforting? Am I showing care and concern? Will my words relate how much I love this person? Am I speaking because I feel obligated? Will my words be directed toward myself in a self-centered way? Is my pride getting in the way of genuine love?"

If what you say is genuine, sincere, and truthful, it will show in your actions.

A simple equation:

words = action
actions = words

They should be the same: a perfect match

Dear children, let us not love in words and tongues but with action and in truth.

(1 John 3:18)

Be aware of your own limitations; you may lack the time or have other responsibilities. No one has the capabilities to help everyone who needs comfort, support, and help. But the body of Christ, your church, does. Look for ways to show love to your brothers and sisters who are grieving. Take a leadership role in leading other members of your church to help others.

Each member of your church has a different gift; encourage them to use their individual gifts. Paul said it best in Romans:

[So] in Christ we who are many from one body, and each member belongs to all the others. We have different gifts, according to the grace given us.

(Romans 12:5-6a)

The gifts Paul is speaking about are serving, teaching, encouraging, giving, leading, and showing mercy. Each gift fulfils a need for those grieving. What is your gift, and how can you use it to help those grieving? When will you reach out to them?

Peter reminds us:

Above all, love each other deeply, because love covers over a multitude of sins. Offer hospitality to one another without grumbling. Each one should use whatever gift he has received to serve others, faithfully administering God's grace in its various forms. If anyone speaks, he should do it as one speaking the very words of God. If anyone serves, he should do it with the strength God provides, so that in all things God may be praised through Jesus Christ.

To him be the glory and the power forever and ever. Amen.

(1 Peter 4:8-11)

Grieving people's physical health must also be considered. Encourage them to eat nutritious food on a regular schedule. You may want to bring food already prepared for them to eat. If you do, consider staying and eating with them. It is not enjoyable to eat alone. There is also the option of going out to eat. Offer to go get groceries for them. Encourage them to get adequate sleep. A routine bedtime is beneficial. Observe their appearance. If it looks like they are not taking care of personal grooming, ask how you can help.

Try to get them involved in the things they used to do. You can also suggest new things. Include them in your social activities. Call frequently, especially in the evening. Send cards, even weeks after the funeral, and include a little note in them. This makes it personal and shows you care. (I received so many cards the week of the funeral and the week after, and then, all of a sudden, no more cards.)

When you visit, bring a movie you can watch together. Bring a book, magazine, or flowers from your garden. Offer to do some minor repairs or other tasks. Things that are difficult for some are cleaning out the gutters, raking leaves, mowing the lawn, doing laundry, cleaning house, maintaining the car, and others. Of course, it depends on whether those grieving are male or female, how old they are, etc. You know them, and you know what help they need.

There will come a time when it will be necessary for those grieving to take on more responsibility for themselves. You may need to step back a little. Let them know that you will always be available. You are only a phone call away. It will be necessary to encourage the grievers to start rebuilding their lives and to start experiencing new things, all while getting back to normal activities. It is time for them to get involved with others by taking the initiative to reach out to others. You know them and what they enjoy doing. Let them know that you will still be available and still want to be part of their lives. Your goal now is for them to take control and assume responsibility for their own healing and recovery. Stay in touch, monitoring their progress. Remember the things you did that helped in the past; if necessary, resume some of these for a time. Always encourage them to seek answers from God's Word; strength, hope, comfort, joy, peace, contentment, healing, and growing are all part of God's plan for those grieving.

In the previous section, "You, the Grieving Person," there are many ways for those grieving to help themselves. This will give you some suggestions as you help the griever(s) you have reached out to.

May God bring many blessings to you for your faithful commitment to helping and caring for one of his grieving children.

Part VIII

Plan of Salvation

God's Plan of Salvation

*R*ealize that God loves you.

For God so loved the world that He gave His only begotten son, that whosoever believeth in Him should not perish but have everlasting life.
(John 3:16)

The Bible says that all men are sinners:

For all have sinned and come short of the Glory of God.
(Romans 3:23)

God's Word also says that sin must be paid for:

For the wages of sin is death.
(Romans 6:23)

The good news is that Christ paid for our sins:

But God demonstrates his own love for us in this: While we were still sinners, Christ died for us.
(Romans 5:8)

Pray and receive Christ as your Savior:

[F]or, "Everyone who calls upon the name of the LORD shall be saved.
(Romans 10:13)

If you have made this decision, please seek out a pastor, minister, clergy member, or friend who can rejoice with you and encourage you in your new walk with Christ.